THE LITTLE BOOK OF
WHITTLING

BY CHRIS LUBKEMANN

FOX CHAPEL
PUBLISHING

© 2005, 2013 by Fox Chapel Publishing Company, Inc.

The Little Book of Whittling, ISBN 978-1-56523-772-8, is a re-printing of *The Little Book of Whittling,* ISBN 978-1-56523-274-7, first published in 2005 by Fox Chapel Publishing. No part of this book may be duplicated for resale or distribution under any circumstances. Any such copying is a violation of copyright law.

PHOTOGRAPHY: Greg Heisey

ISBN 978-1-56523-772-8

Library of Congress Cataloging-in-Publication Data

Lubkemann, Chris.
  The little book of whittling / Chris Lubkemann.
     pages cm
  ISBN 978-1-56523-772-8
  1. Wood-carving. 2. Wood-carving--Technique. I. Title.
  TT199.7.L822 2013
  736'.4--dc23
                              2012031297

To learn more about the other great books from
Fox Chapel Publishing, or to find a retailer near you,
call toll-free 800-457-9112 or visit us at
www.FoxChapelPublishing.com.

Printed in China
Eleventh printing

Note to Authors: We are always looking for talented
authors to write new books in our area of woodworking, design,
and related crafts. Please send a brief letter describing your idea to
Acquisition Editor, 1970 Broad Street, East Petersburg, PA 17520.

Lovingly Dedicated

To Mom, who was, without a doubt, the greatest fan of my work. (Who else would dedicate permanent space in her purse to a little plastic display box of my carvings?!)

To Dad, whose tools and readily shared raw materials inspired me early on in my great appreciation and enjoyment of working with wood.

Acknowledgments

If you ever want to have fun and a great experience working on a book, do one with the folks at Fox Chapel. Many were involved in the production of this book and to all who contributed I say a huge "Thank You!"

I'd especially like to single out Alan, Peg, Gretchen, Troy, Mark, and Greg. They're the ones I had the most contact with.

While I consider myself at least fairly proficient in my knowledge and experience with what is explained in this book as related to wood and the use of a pocketknife, I can't claim expertise in all aspects of hiking, camping, s'more-making, and camp recipes. For these super-interesting little additions, hints, and notes that are scattered throughout the book and which add so much to it, all credit goes to Gretchen and her "Fox Chapel Hikers Gang" (to coin a new name) for their great contribution.

It's been a fun team to work with!

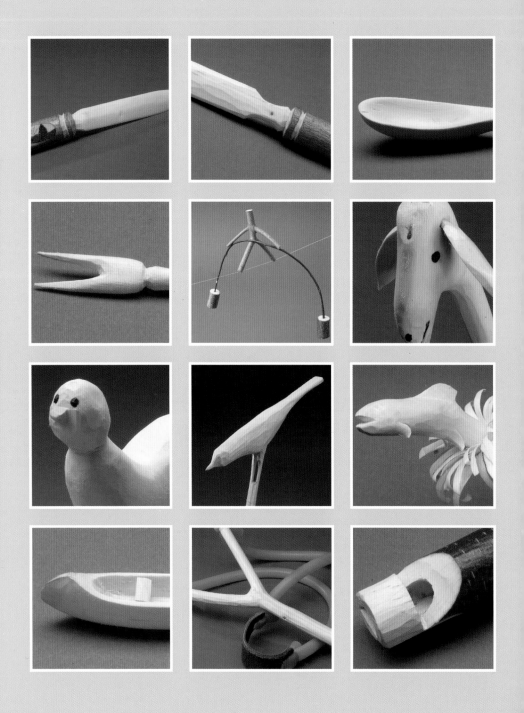

Contents

The Projects

CHRIS LUBKEMANN

A child of missionaries, Chris Lubkemann grew up in the forests of Brazil and Peru, where sawing, planing, hammering, and building were a part of daily life. He quickly developed an appreciation for wood and entertained himself—and others—by handcrafting rafts, tree houses, traps, and slingshots from scrap wood. Since that time, he has continued to integrate his woodworking skills with good old-fashioned fun.

Chris's first writing on whittling appeared in 1972 in the form of published notes, which have since been produced in both English and Portuguese. His most recent book, *Whittling Twigs and Branches*, was published by Fox Chapel Publishing in 2002. Chris is also a regular contributor to *Chip Chats* magazine. His work has been featured in *Wood Carving Illustrated* magazine and on the DIY network. He has carved some of the world's smallest branch carvings, and his smallest branch rooster was given a Guinness World Record Certificate in 1981.

Currently, Chris demonstrates whittling as the resident woodcarver at the Amish Farm and House in Lancaster, Pennsylvania.

whit•tle (hwĭt'l, wĭt'l) *v.* -tling
To pare small bits or shavings from (wood) with a knife.

INTRODUCTION

For many people, "whittling" conjures up quite a colorful image. It goes something like this: a fairly old codger with longish hair, wearing bib overalls and missing about a third of his teeth, sits in an old bentwood rocker on the front porch of a very weathered cabin located somewhere up in "them thar hills"—or several old codgers sit on stools around an old potbellied iron stove in the corner of a 125-year-old country store. In either case, there are piles of random wood shavings and chips in front of each stool or chair. Most importantly, there are the old, well-worn pocketknives and the even older and more worn hands that wield them. Go on—fill in the picture with even more details.

I'm sure a lot of whittling has indeed been done in the molds just described. And who is to say that some real benefits haven't come from those front porch or round-the-stove sessions? While it's probably true that in many cases all that was produced was a pile of chips and shavings with nothing but the knife left in the hands, I'm sure that on many other occasions what remained in the hand opposite the one holding the knife was an incredible work of art.

With these connotations of whittling and whittlers, it is easy to see why many whittlers/woodcarvers try too hard to define and to run away from certain terms. I've come across a number of folks in the woodcarving community who struggle with the word "whittle" and opt for the word "carve" because they

> Throughout this book, you'll notice tip boxes just like this one. Inside you'll find information meant to add to your whittling experience—anything from methods for starting a fire to baits for fishing to recipes for the perfect s'mores. Also keep your eye out for little tips and facts at the bottom of many pages. Whether you're on the trail, in camp, or at home, I hope that these tidbits evoke the fun and relaxing atmosphere that the ideal whittling experience will create. Oh, and be sure to check out some of my favorite tips on pages 32 and 33!

want their work to be taken as serious art and not as the production of wood chips. Just for fun, I went to the dictionary that was closest at hand to see how it defined the word "whittle". Here's what I found: "to pare or cut off chips from the surface of (wood) with a knife" or "to shape or form by so paring or cutting." I also looked up "carve": "to make or shape by or as by cutting, chipping, hewing" and "to decorate the surface of with cut figures or designs." Sounds like "whittle" and "carve" could almost be synonyms! True, the first definition of "whittle" could lend itself to the final product being just a pile of random chips on the floor, but the second definition certainly allows for all kinds of creativity and objects of genuine art.

Today, whittling is alive and well and is certainly not limited to the characters, settings, or descriptions I've listed above. I would describe whittling as a simple type of woodcarving that involves a knife as its primary instrument. People of all ages, lifestyles, and levels of experience have enjoyed trying this simple and relaxing form of carving. Folks who have never carved a piece of wood will discover a new source of fun and satisfaction. Even old hands at woodcarving may find a few ideas that they'll get a charge out of.

Aside from its relaxing effect, whittling has a number of other advantages. To start, the main raw material is free and, generally speaking, quite easy to find. (I don't ever recall having to pay even a cent for one of the twigs or branches I've used over the past 39 years!) And as for the tools required and the few other materials and supplies, they're simple, inexpensive, and very easy to get.

Also, whittling in general is a very "portable" craft. You can take it just about anywhere. That's why I've designed this book as an outdoor companion. Whether you're on the trail, sitting around the campfire, or just relaxing on the front porch, you'll find lots of interesting facts, games, recipes, and more to keep you occupied between whittling projects. If you're not as inclined to the outdoors, you can take your whittling to a number of indoor locations as well. I've whittled at commencement exercises, at wedding receptions, in barbershops, in doctor's offices, and during totally stopped traffic jams, just to name a few.

So, relax, carve away, whittle, shape, form, whatever. Enjoy what you're doing, and don't worry if your finished project doesn't turn out perfect or about any preconceived notions of whittling. My hope is that you'll jump into the projects that follow and that they will provide you with fun, relaxation, and creativity and will "prime the pump" for other projects that this particular whittler has never even thought of!

Whittling is a very portable craft—you can take it just about anywhere. As you can see, it was a perfect way to pass the time while I was stuck in totally stopped traffic on I-81 in Virginia.

Happy Whittling!
Chris Lubkemann

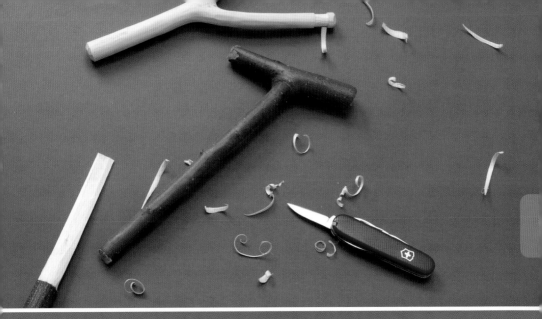

GETTING STARTED

For those of you who have never whittled before, take some time to read through the following sections for some tips and techniques that will make your whittling easier and more enjoyable. Some of the topics we'll cover include choosing your wood, sharpening, and the basic cuts.

CHOOSING WOOD

While the main raw material we'll be using and illustrating in the following chapters generally consists of small branches or twigs of one description or another, I definitely don't mean to imply that only branches will work for these projects. Actually, many kinds of scrap wood will serve the same purposes. I choose twigs and branches because I, having been a "branch carver" most of my life, happen to have a ton of twigs and branches on hand and they're more what I'm used to carving.

If you don't have immediate access to any good branches but do have a supply of milled wood scraps, go ahead and experiment with

what you have. Make sure any milled lumber you use is straight-grained and without knots. Just to show you some of the possibilities, the photo below shows different types of wood along with two letter openers and a little boat that emerged from milled scraps. Generally speaking, however, I'd still recommend twigs and branches as an excellent raw material.

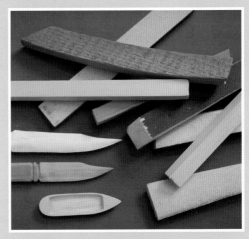

If you don't have immediate access to good branches, milled scraps are a fine alternative.

GENERAL CHARACTERISTICS OF GOOD WOOD

Most of the projects on the following pages call for straight, "unforked" pieces of wood. As a rule, the best woods (1) are straight-grained, (2) have a small pith (the small spongy part right in the center of the branch), and (3) don't have sticky sap to contend with.

A quick note about pine: For the most part, I avoid using pine branches because it forces me to deal with a lot of sticky sap. If I carved fresh pine, I'd be spending an awful lot of time cleaning my knife and my hands. However, some milled pine blocks or board scraps will work for several of the projects in this book. There's nothing quite like experience to show you what will work well and what won't.

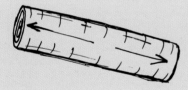

Most of the projects in this book call for straight, unforked branches. Notice that the grain runs in only one direction.

Sometimes it's an advantage to use a forked branch. These branches are a little trickier to carve because the grain runs in three different directions.

MOISTURE IN BRANCHES

As you are looking for branches, it's best to avoid wood that is so dry that the branch snaps cleanly in two when bent. I prefer to carve wood that has at least a little bit of moisture in it. As a rule of thumb, look for wood that is neither freshly cut nor very dry.

Some of the hardwoods, such as various maples, oaks, and beeches, need to be worked when they're still quite fresh. Some of the birches—with the notable exception of black birch, which is harder than other varieties—carve nicely when they've dried out a bit. This is especially true for some of the very thin birch twigs used for carving the smallest miniatures.

To keep branches from drying out too much, I cut them up into ready-to-carve sizes and store them in plastic bags in the freezer. Of course, this assumes that you can negotiate with your family's freezer administrator for wood storage space!

In many instances, you can soak branches that have become too hard and too dry. Once the branch has soaked, treat the wood as if it were a freshly cut branch, letting it redry some before working it. One problem to look out for is bark that will loosen and deteriorate after soaking. Often, it's better to look for a more ideal branch rather than soak a branch. Don't make more work for yourself than you have to.

The pith—the spongy part in the center of a branch—should be small. For instance, a 1/2"-diameter branch should have a pith that is 1/16" in diameter or smaller.

LOCATING BRANCHES

Finding good branches to carve is a large part of the fun of the whole process. With a bit of time and practice, one develops a well-honed instinct for good wood. You'll notice it on the side of the road, next to trash cans on pick-up day, in piles next to new construction sites, lying all over the place after windstorms, and in piles at recycling plants. Of course, many folks have a decent supply right in their own yards. I always have a little saw or pruning shears in my van so, at a moment's notice, I can take advantage of any good branch find!

WHEN TO CUT BRANCHES

For the most part, any time of the year is a good time to cut wood. Even winter is great because it's easy to spot the best-shaped branches. And, if you happen to be tramping through a frozen-over New Jersey swamp looking for a swamp maple (which, by the way, grows in a lot of places besides swamps), you can walk on solid footing. Another cold-weather advantage is that if you're branch hunting in rattlesnake or cottonmouth country, the snakes are asleep. That's definitely a plus! In the summer, it's not a bad idea to keep one eye looking for branches and the other eye on the lookout for whatever might be crawling nearby.

PREPARING THE BRANCHES

Sometimes the branches you find will have an accumulation of dust or even some kind of mold or natural fungus. A good rag or brush and a bucket of water will solve the problem. It's definitely better to work with clean wood. Often, the very first thing I'll do with a particular batch of branches is wash off the bark so that no dirt gets transferred to the clean inside wood.

WOOD SPECIES

Naturally, some varieties of wood work better than others, but it's not always possible to have the ideal wood at hand. Just experiment with the kinds of branches you collect. Chances are pretty good that you'll find at least one kind of tree or bush that does the trick, and, before long, you'll develop your own list of favorite raw materials.

Most of the 80 or so kinds of branches I've used have been hardwoods. To be honest, I really haven't liked working with softwoods very much. Since most of the branches I carve are on the greenish side and are relatively small, the hardness of the wood hasn't been a deterrent at all. The following list includes just a few of my favorites.

BIRCH: Any variety of birch is excellent. I've never met a bad birch yet! The birches are among my all-time favorite woods.

MAPLE: There are quite a few varieties of maple, too. Some have a very small pith, and others have a larger pith. For most projects, the smaller-pith variety works better. Just experiment. Any maple is worth trying. Swamp maple is one of my favorites.

CHERRY: I've carved several kinds of cherry, both domesticated and wild. All are quite good.

BEECH: I've found that beech can be a bit brittle, but if you're careful, it works fine.

OAK: There are many varieties of oak, some much better than others for certain projects. I've made some nice pieces from pin oak, live oak, and water oak. Red oak is not particularly good for most of these projects because it tends to have a very open grain that's kind of wavy.

HOLLY: A very hard, close-grained wood that produces some beautiful pieces.

ORANGE, LEMON, TANGERINE, GRAPEFRUIT: All of the citrus woods are good (except for the new, fast-growing shoots, which tend to be very pithy). I remember getting some great citrus branches when a Sarasota citrus grove was replaced by a school. There's always pruning time, too, when lots of branches are on the ground.

CEDAR: One of the few evergreen trees I've used. There's a bit of sap to contend with, but nothing like with fresh pine branches!

MYRTLE: I think the kind I used was wax myrtle, but other varieties are worth trying, too.

BOTTLEBRUSH, INDIAN ROSEWOOD, VIBURNUM: Several Florida woods that work well. One of my all-time favorite slingshot forks is viburnum—very, very strong and beautifully symmetrical!

FLOWERING CRABAPPLE, FLOWERING PLUM: Ornamental trees that have good branches.

APPLE, PEACH, QUINCE, GUAVA: Other fruit trees that have good branches to work with.

CHOOSING A KNIFE

As far as tools are concerned, I'll have to admit that I'm probably somewhat of a minimalist. My main tool is a two-bladed pocketknife. Of course, the Victorinox Swiss Army Tinker I've been using for the past several years has a few more gadgets on it than I typically employ for carving (though I do use them a lot for other jobs), but I have found it to be one of my favorite blades. The small blade of the pocketknife performs 90% of the operations, and the larger blade the other 10%.

Plenty of people have used typical carving knives successfully. It's a good idea to have at least two blades: one should be no longer than 1 1/2 inches, and the other should be between 2 and 2 1/2 inches long. The type of knife you choose is ultimately a matter of personal preference, so choose a knife that you are the most comfortable using.

Whatever knife or knife blades you use, make sure you keep in mind the following ten extremely important rules of carving. Don't leave any of them out!

1 1/2 inch blade is used 90% of the time

2 to 2 1/2 inch blade is used 10% of the time

TEN EXTREMELY IMPORTANT RULES OF CARVING

1 Make sure your knife is sharp.

2 Your knife must be really sharp!

3 Don't try carving with a knife that isn't sharp.

4 Before starting to carve, check your knife to see if it's sharp.

5 Carving with a less-than-very-sharp knife is very frustrating!

6 In the realm of woodcarving, sharp is *good*, dull is *bad*.

7 *Keep* your knife sharp!

8 If your knife is really sharp, it will cut much better.

9 If you missed the point of Rules 1 through 8, *make sure the knife you carve with is sharp!*

10 If there's any remaining doubt, refer back to Rules 1 through 9.

OTHER TOOLS AND SUPPLIES

Besides a knife, you may find that there are a few other tools that will make your carving more enjoyable. I'll cover some of the ones that I use, but be sure to customize the list based on your personal preferences.

SANDPAPER. Choose a number of different grits in the fine to very fine range. You'll often use sandpaper to smooth out the projects.

PENCIL, PEN, OR MARKER. Any of these instruments will work well for sketching your designs on the wood.

ROTARY TOOL OR OTHER WOODCARVING TOOLS. Rotary tools, chisels, drills, and other similar instruments can speed up some of the projects. These types of tools are certainly not necessary, but feel free to use them if you have them.

CYANOACRYLATE (CA) GLUE. If you seal some of the projects with CA glue before painting, it will give them added strength. It will also allow you to use water-based paints on parts that would otherwise "uncurl," such as flower petals.

WOODBURNER. This tool is one of my favorites for personalizing projects with names, dates, and designs.

OIL OR ACRYLIC PAINTS. Oil paints won't uncurl petals, and therefore does not require a coat of CA glue before using. Acrylics work well, especially in conjunction with CA glue, and they are much easier to clean up than oil paints.

CLEAR FINISH. Some projects don't call for any finish, but polyurethane can be a good choice when you'd like to protect your piece.

SHARPENING AND HONING

There are all kinds of methods and devices for sharpening knives. I will share with you my own very simple sharpening system, but feel free to experiment and find what works best for you.

Like any method or system, mine takes a little practice, but it does work, and I've been satisfied with it for quite a few years. The price is pretty good, too—practically nothing, after a very small initial investment.

If I'm starting out with a totally dull knife (even a new blade can be dull), I usually use my

Sharpening tools (left to right): leather strop with stropping compound, various grits of wet-or-dry sandpaper, block for the sandpaper, and two different double-sided sharpening stones.

Go through the grits—from coarser to finer. I usually use 320, 400, and 600.

two-sided sharpening stone to get the process started—first the coarser surface and then the finer. (Most sharpening stones have two surfaces.) With the blade not quite flat against the stone, I use a circular motion followed up by several slicing motions. After this part, the blade is semi-sharp, but not yet ready for carving.

Then I'll go to a series of little strips of wet-or-dry sandpaper or emery cloth—like the kind used on auto body work. The three grits that I generally use are 320, 400, and 600 (the higher the number, the finer the grit). Some of my little beat-up sheets have been around for eight or ten years and are still working! They're virtually paper-smooth, but they still serve to polish the blade's edge.

Finally, I'll end up stropping (wiping) my blade on a piece of leather, usually with a little bit of stropping compound. For many years, I just used the rough backside of an old leather belt.

If I'm starting with a blade that only needs a touch of sharpening, I'll start with the finest grit of wet-or-dry sandpaper and finish with a few strops on the leather.

2 With the blade not quite flat, move it across the coarse side of the stone using a circular motion. Then, make a few slicing motions across the stone. Don't lift or turn the blade as it goes across the stone. Flip to the finer (yellow) side and repeat the same steps.

3 Using wet-or-dry sandpaper on top of a block of wood, use the same sharpening motions you used in Step 2. Be sure to turn the blade around to get both sides.

5 Even if your pieces of sandpaper are virtually smooth, they'll still work to polish the edge of the blade.

6 Apply a little bit of stropping compound to your leather strop. With the blade flat against the strop, stroke it *away* from the edge a few times on each side.

THE BASIC CUTTING STROKES

There are several ways to cut with a knife. The three particular strokes described here are illustrated for right-handed carvers. Left-handers, of course, will reverse the hands, following a mirror image of the illustrations.

STRAIGHTAWAY CUTTING

This cut is good for removing a lot of wood or bark quickly. Hold the wood in your left hand, and using long, firm strokes, cut away from yourself with your right hand. I find that when I use this stroke my right wrist is pretty well locked, not bending during the cutting stroke.

DRAWCUTTING

This technique involves placing the wood in your left hand and the knife in your right. Cut toward yourself (sort of like peeling an orange) with short strokes, using your right thumb as a brace against the wood. Be sure to keep some wood between the blade and your thumb. I find it helpful (and much safer!) to keep my right thumb braced on my left thumb, not on top of the wood itself. That way, I don't run the risk of the blade coming up into my right thumb on its follow-through when it suddenly clears the end of the wood.

THUMBPUSHING

This particular stroke is extremely practical for small cuts where precise control is needed and you don't want to overcut. Hold the wood in the four fingers of your left hand, leaving your left thumb free. Grip the knife in your right hand, keeping your right thumb against the back of the blade. With your left thumb, push either the back of the blade or the back of your right thumb.

Now that you've been through the basics, let's go ahead and attack the projects. The reason I've placed the knife first is that many of the pieces that follow it will borrow some of the same strokes and techniques. Here's hoping you'll have all kinds of fun and even add five or six (or ten) more projects of your own!

GETTING STARTED

KNIFE

MATERIALS:
- Knife (Remember, sharp!)
- Straight-grained wood of choice
- Sandpaper for smoothing the blade—a couple of grits on the fine to very fine side (150- and 220-grit would work). Well-worn pieces of sandpaper are great for supersmooth fine-tuning!
- Cyanoacrylate glue for hardening the edge of the blade
- Polyurethane or some other clear finish to coat the knife
- Pencil, pen, or marker
- Woodburner (optional)

Knives have been some of my quickest spontaneous carving projects wherever I happen to be with my pocketknife. (You can also use this project as a letter opener.) It's usually not hard to find a straight stick or scrap of wood lying around. Naturally, it's better if the stick or scrap of milled wood is free of knots and is straight-grained.

As for the efficiency and usefulness of a well-made wooden knife, let me assure you that wood can indeed be shaped and sharpened into a very good blade. When I was a kid in the Amazon rain forests of Brazil and Peru, the majority of the arrowheads that the native tribespeople made were carved of wood, and they really worked! Anyway, I figure that if the very self-sufficient hunters and fishers that survived for countless generations in the jungles of Brazil and Peru hunted and fished with wooden points, I'm sure we can make a usable knife! Of course, a wooden knife or letter opener will never be able to do what a steel knife can do, but it will have a variety of uses.

Keep in mind that you can modify many of the projects' sizes, and this project is no exception. The techniques are basically the same for any size, whether it's one inch long or two feet long. The two basic components of each knife will be 1) the handle and 2) the blade. There are also a tremendous variety of shapes, styles, and designs in carving the handles. Blades, too, can have quite a few different shapes, depending in part on the shape of the original "blank" branch or piece of wood used.

KNIFE

1 Choose a relatively smooth branch (as few knots as possible) with a small pith. If you're using a scrap of lumber, make sure it's straight-grained. The two branches on the left are birch, and the two on the right are maple.

2 This particular branch is slightly curved when held like this, but when it is rotated one-quarter of a turn, it is basically straight. The straight view shows the top of the knife (inset). The curved view shows the side profile of the knife.

3 Round the butt of the handle. Remember, if you're using a drawcutting stroke, keep your thumb behind and below the piece of wood you're cutting. That way, when the blade makes that quick little follow-through jump after taking off a chip of wood, it won't do minor surgery on your thumb!

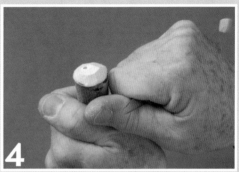

4 Here's the rounded end of the handle, with the knife blade having completed its follow-through. I think the little blurry chip above my hand is the last little chip that jumped off the blade.

A Slice of History

Master Cutler Karl Elsener began making multi-functional knives for the Swiss army in 1891. The Swiss name for the knife was "Offiziermesser," but it quickly became known as the "Swiss Army Knife" by the American GI's who used it during World War II. Today, the company makes over 100 different models of pocketknives, and the flagship model is featured in the Museum of Modern Art for its excellence in design.

5

After deciding how long you want the handle and how long you want the blade to be, begin flattening the sides of the branch where the blade will be, using long, straight strokes.

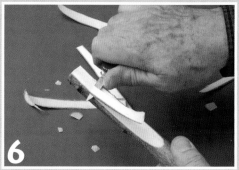

6

I find I can get a good long stroke if I lock my wrist and push the knife all the way to the end of the branch.

7

Take thin slices so you don't overcut. It's definitely better to cut a little at a time than to gouge out a large slice that takes you deeper than you want to go.

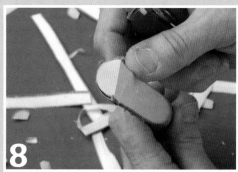

8

Stop before you get into the pith in the center of the branch.

9

Flatten the opposite side of the branch, making sure you start your cut at the same point where you began flattening the first side.

10

Top view of the blade after both sides are flattened.

KNIFE

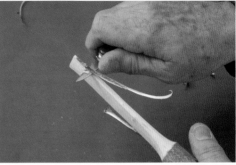

11 Remove the remaining little strips of bark from the top and bottom of the blade.

12 Sketch the blade shape you'd like your knife to have.

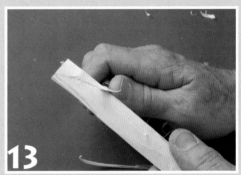

13 Remove wood to form the bottom of the point of the blade.

14 Take off the top of the point, using a slight scooping stroke.

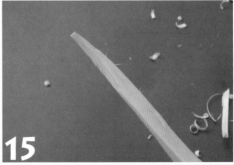

15 Here's what the point of the blade looks like so far, looking down at the top side of the knife.

16

Sharpen the blade edge. If the branch you're using is still fairly fresh, don't sharpen the edge too much. Let the wood dry a bit and firm up before you do your finer sharpening.

17

Make a fairly wide V-cut at the base of the blade where it joins the handle. Be sure not to make the blade/handle junction too thin. Remember, this is wood, not steel, and you want the knife to be strong enough to be truly functional.

18

Usually, I chip carve a little grooved ring at both ends of the handle. Not that it makes the knife work any better—it just looks better. And if you really want to get creative, the handle is where you can go for broke with your chip carving, taking advantage of the contrast between the darker bark and the lighter wood underneath.

KNIFE

19

Often, I take a swatch out of one or both sides of the handle. Note the directions of these cuts. Cut toward the center of the swatch from both ends so that the cuts meet in the middle. Don't try to scoop out the whole piece in one direction.

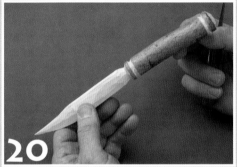

20

On this particular knife, I left the bark on one side of the handle.

21

Once the wood has dried enough to allow for sanding, smooth the blade with a bit of fine sandpaper.

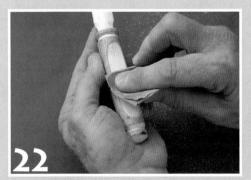

22

Smooth the handle swatch, too.

23

You can really fine-tune and sharpen the blade with some very fine sandpaper.

24

To harden the blade edge and the point of the knife, run cyanoacrylate (CA) glue along the edge and on the point.

25

When the CA glue hardens, resand the edge and point to the sharpness you want. At this point, your knife is complete, but you can customize it as I have.

A Knife that Goes Far Beyond Whittling

A good quality pocketknife has unlimited uses. The knife used in this book is the Victorinox Swiss Army Tinker. It is relatively inexpensive, and its uses on or off the trail go way beyond whittling.

Features include:

- Large knife blade
- Small knife blade
- Phillips screwdriver
- Large screwdriver
- Small screwdriver
- Bottle opener
- Tweezers
- Can opener
- Wire stripper
- Reamer/punch
- Plastic toothpick

26

Woodburning a scene and a name on the handle. The possibilities at this point are almost endless!

27

Permanent markers work well for adding color.

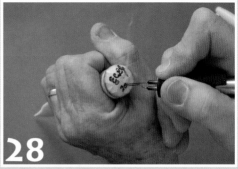

28

Always sign and date your piece.

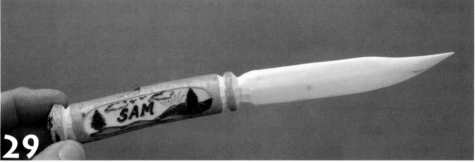

29

Done!...Well, almost. I always put some kind of finish on the whole knife when it's completed. Any polyurethane will work, as will any clear acrylic. The polyurethane finishes are harder, but the acrylics are faster drying. Take your pick. The finish keeps it cleaner, especially if it is going to be used. And there's really no good reason why it shouldn't be!

A whole slew of finished knives and letter openers! Note the different handles, a number of them incorporating knots. The little letter opener with the heart on the handle was a special piece I made for my wife one Valentine's Day.

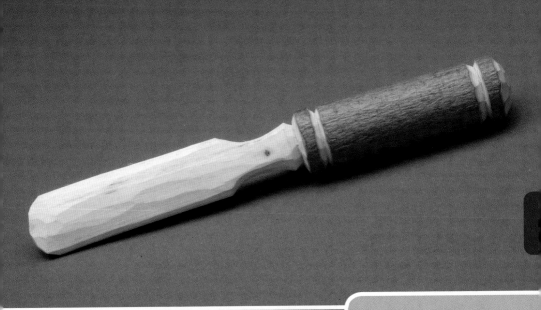

SPREADER

MATERIALS:

- Knife
- Straight-grained wood of choice
- Sandpaper—a couple of grits on the fine to very fine side (150- and 220-grit would work).
- Polyurethane or other clear finish of choice (optional)

Whether you're at home or on the trail, this spreader is a better alternative to a knife, and especially to plastic utensils, when you're looking to add condiments to your favorite food. Customize the handle and the blade for jam or jelly on your morning toast, peanut butter for your sandwiches, cream cheese on your bagels, or mustard for your hot dogs. All you need is a little piece of wood or a small branch and your handy pocketknife, and in just a few minutes, you'll be set with a great spreader.

Most of the steps in carving a spreading utensil will be almost identical to those used in producing a knife. The differences will come in the shaping of the blade or "spreader" part of the piece. If you're customizing this project, look to make the handle fit comfortably in your hand and to make the blade fit what you'll be spreading.

SPREADER

Several spreader possibilities and five spreader "blanks."

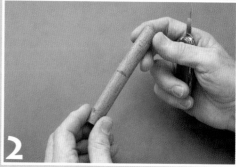

I've picked the largest of the five, a little maple branch.

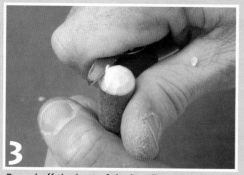

Round off the butt of the handle.

Old-Fashioned Mustard

Without the condiments to dress up the classic fire-roasted hot dogs, open-flamed burgers, or morning toast, camping cuisine would be pretty dull. So put that spreader to use.

Ingredients:

- 1/2 cup white vinegar
- 1/2 cup dry mustard
- 1/4 cup water
- 3/4 cup brown sugar
- 2 eggs beaten

In saucepan, mix vinegar and mustard. Stir in remaining ingredients and bring to a slow boil over low heat, stirring constantly. Cook and stir until thickened, about 10 minutes. Store in the refrigerator until you're ready to take on the trail.

Cut a little V-shaped groove around the end of the handle.

5 Cut another groove farther down the handle, just a bit above where you want the blade of the spreader to start.

6 Flatten the blade of the spreader from both sides.

7 This is what the spreader will look like from the end.

Sun-Dried Tomato Mayonnaise

Next time you're having a burger out on the trail, try this delicious mayonnaise instead of ketchup. And, once you have the right tools, it's easy to spread.

Combine:

- 1/2 cup mayonnaise
- 2 teaspoons minced sun-dried tomatoes
- 1 teaspoon Italian seasoning
- 1 teaspoon lemon juice (preferably fresh)
- 1 teaspoon sugar
- Minced garlic (add as much or as little as you like)

SPREADER

SPREADER

8

Using both thumbpushing and drawcutting cuts, always cutting toward the center, narrow the neck of the spreader—the part between the handle and the actual blade.

9

Slightly round the end of the blade.

10

Here's where the spreader stands at this point.

11

Make another little V-cut groove between the neck and the handle.

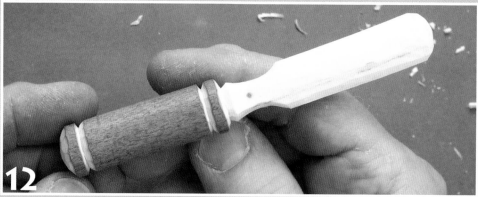

12

Done, except for sanding and finishing. As with the knife, sand the spreader smooth. Even a little one-inch-square piece of fine sandpaper will do the trick. I personally prefer not to put any finish on my spreaders. Generally, I think wooden cooking and serving utensils are best left as unfinished wood. However, if you'd prefer to finish your cooking utensils, I recommend salad bowl finish; it puts a nice shine on the wood without including any toxic ingredients. If you use salad bowl finish, make sure you allow the utensil 24 hours of drying time to evaporate any chemicals from the piece.

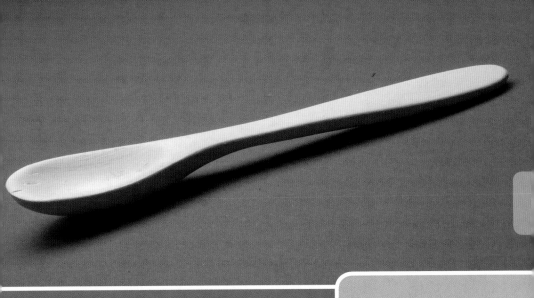

SPOON

MATERIALS:

- Knife
- Straight-grained wood of choice
- Sandpaper—a couple of grits on the fine to very fine side (150- and 220-grit would work).
- Polyurethane or other clear finish of choice (optional)
- Pencil, pen, or marker
- Rotary tool (optional)

It's true what they say—necessity is the mother of invention. This particular project came about when I was set up at a craft show and was getting ready to eat my lunch. As I opened my lunchbox that my wife, Sheri, had so thoughtfully packed for me, I remember being a bit puzzled as to how I was going to eat my yogurt without any spoon. (While good food was on the menu, evidently utensils were not.) Since eating my yogurt with my very, very sharp pocketknife was not the most attractive option, I instead used the knife to carve a five- or six-inch branch into a workable spoon. My yogurt was duly enjoyed, and the spoon is still in one of my little carry-around boxes, waiting for another chance to bail me out of a spoonless situation.

There are a tremendous variety of spoon styles, shapes, and sizes. Several are shown at the end of this chapter. The very small, miniature spoons remind me of the old-time salt dippers that were used to dish out salt from little salt bowls. The size of the spoon you make will of course depend on the size of the blank piece of wood you start out with. You can aim for a smaller mustard or relish spoon or a mammoth pot-stirring spoon for the camp cook. The one I'll be showing in the following sequence is a fairly simple teaspoon-size one...practical for yogurt, you might say!

1 Pick a straight, knot-free branch, one just a bit longer than you want your spoon to be.

2 This birch branch has a diameter roughly that of a quarter.

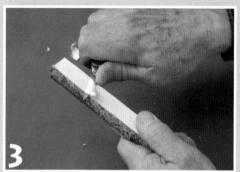

3 Flatten one side of the branch along the entire length of the branch, using long, firm strokes. This side will be the top of the spoon.

4 Some folks feel comfortable with a drawing stroke.

5 Using a slightly scooping stroke, flatten the bottom of the handle, leaving the end of the branch thick for making the bowl of the spoon.

6 Draw the basic shape of the spoon.

7

Shape the handle. Remember, always cut toward the center of the branch when you do any curved, scooping cuts. If you cut out from the center, chances are good that you'll split the wood where you don't want to.

8

Continue to gradually shape the handle. This view shows the underside.

9

Remove bark from the bowl part of the branch.

10

Here's where the spoon is at this point.

SOME THINGS JUST GO TOGETHER

Whittling on the front porch would not be complete without a tall, cool glass of lemonade, and this recipe is a classic:

Ingredients:

- 2 teaspoons lemon zest
- 2 cups sugar
- 1/2 cup water
- 1 cup freshly squeezed lemons (6 lemons)

Bring lemon zest, sugar, and water to a boil for 30 seconds. Remove from heat and add the lemon juice. Cool to room temperature and keep cool in refrigerator.

Fill glass with ice. Pour 1/4 cup of syrup and top with cool water. Substitute club soda or seltzer for a fizzy version.

Garnish with a lemon slice or sprig of mint, if desired.

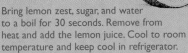

Little Fact: Florida's Waccasassa Bay Preserve State Park shelters numerous rare and endangered species.   **25**

Shape the bowl of the spoon, cutting off whatever lines you've drawn.

Scoop out the bowl slightly, giving it a bit of a concave curve.

The progress so far.

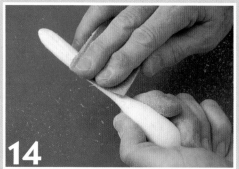

Sand the entire spoon with fine sandpaper. At this point, you'll have a spoon without a hollowed-out bowl.

Draw the perimeter of the inside of the bowl.

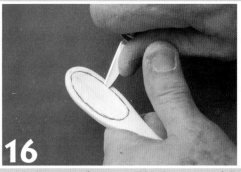

16

With the point of your small blade, very carefully cut inward around the line you've drawn. You can use either a pushing cut or a drawing cut. Chances are that you'll use both. Which one you use will depend on what stroke is more comfortable and easy to control at a given point on your "round trip" around the inside of the bowl. Be very careful to avoid letting your blade slip outward and slice through the outer rim of the bowl.

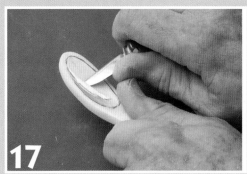
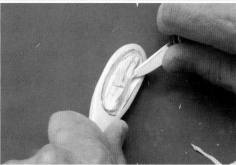

17

Making lots of repeated V-cuts, hollow out the bowl as much as possible. Naturally, with this type of hollowing out, the inside of the bowl is going to be quite rough.

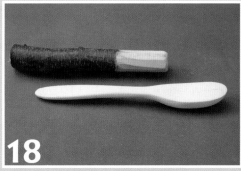

18

Carve yourself a bowl-sanding tool by rounding the end of a branch to a shape that will fit nicely into the bowl of the spoon.

Little Tip: To keep soot off your pots, rub the outsides with a bar of soap.

19 Wrap a bit of sandpaper around the end of the stick, and sand the inside of the bowl.

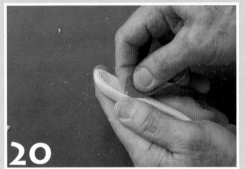

20 There's probably not a more practical tool for fine finish sanding than a little piece of sandpaper held between your thumb and index finger.

21 Of course, if you have a rotary tool, you can shorten the whole bowl-carving process quite a bit. However, I will say that there's a good deal of satisfaction in doing it the more primitive, less high-tech way.

22 To show the finished spoon at work, I borrowed Fox Chapel's pepper shaker. We liked the contrast between the dark pepper and the light spoon. After we shot this photo, I offered Gretchen, my editor, a whole dollar if she would eat the pepper...but she surprisingly "wussed out" on me! Funny thing, some folks don't understand the value of a dollar!

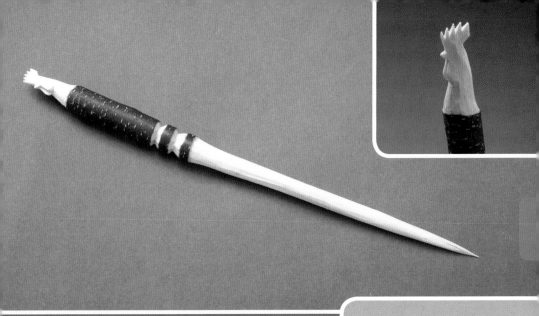

POKER

MATERIALS:
- Knife
- Straight-grained wood of choice
- Sandpaper—a couple of grits on the fine to very fine side (150- and 220-grit would work).
- Polyurethane or other clear finish of choice (optional)

Pokers can come in all lengths and thicknesses, depending on what their intended uses are. You can make a delicate little poker for a single olive or you could conceivably make a six-foot-long one that would serve as a legitimate spear. Just be careful with both sizes! As for design and style, you can go from super simple (just a handle and a point) to very ornate (an intricately carved handle and a fancy stem between the handle and the point). This particular poker will have a rooster head on the handle, just to give it a little more personality, but you can experiment and come up with your own "toppers." For any under-13 carvers that might be trying this project, please understand that I am going on record as clearly stating that this poker (or any of its relatives) is *not* intended as a brother or sister tormentor. In other words, *no sibling poking!*

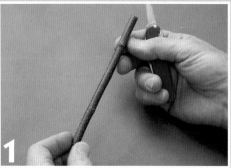

1

We'll start out with a little branch that is straight, is relatively knot-free, and has a small pith.

A CAMPFIRE CLASSIC:

Roasting a Hot Dog over an Open Fire

A longer, slightly larger stick than the one used in this demonstration can make a great hot dog roaster. Once you've finished whittling your poker, grab a hot dog and put your newest creation to good use. If you are going to cook a hot dog over an open flame, it's better to use hot dogs with a natural casing. And, they're excellent when burned...

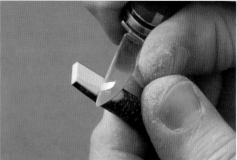

2

Flatten one end of the branch from both sides, stopping short of getting into whatever pith there might be—sort of like you're making the tip of a screwdriver.

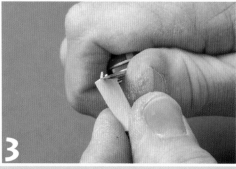

3

After having taken off the two little strips of bark that remain on the "screwdriver tip," slightly curve the top of the tip in order for the rooster's comb to have a bit of a curve itself. Note: Always cut toward the center of the branch, with the cutting strokes meeting in the middle. That way you'll run far less risk of splitting the edge of the branch.

4

Here's what the piece should look like at this stage. The slightly higher end of the arc will be the back of the comb, and the lower part (closer to my thumb) will be the front.

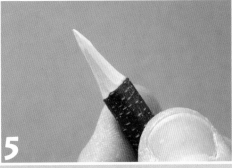

5

Taper the two sides of the now-curved "screwdriver tip." Here we're looking at it from the front.

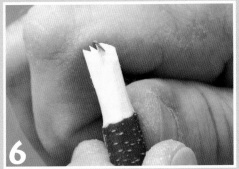

6

Make little sawtooth-type notches for the comb, starting with the back point.

WANT TO DRESS UP THE CLASSIC HOT-DOG-ON-A-STICK?

Grab some cheese, bacon, toothpicks, and your newly whittled poker/skewer...

Without going all the way through, split the hot dog. Tuck strips of cheese into the slit. Wrap the entire hot dog with a slice of bacon and secure it with toothpicks. Roast over an open fire until the bacon is crispy-tender and the hot dog is heated through.

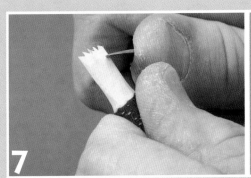

7

To make the front point of the comb and the top of the beak, cut inward from the front. Usually when I make this cut, I wiggle the wood into the knife rather than press the knife into the wood. This technique seems to give better control and keeps me from slicing off several of the previously carved points of the comb.

8

Very carefully shape the back point of the comb and the back of the rooster's neck. This is done by a downward and inward cut from the top and an upward and inward cut from the bottom. Don't try to take this lopsided *V* out in two strokes. Do small, successive cuts until you get the desired depth. I've also tapered the beak from the sides to bring it to a point.

How Did the Hot Dog Get its Name?

History has it that the name "hot dog" was first coined in 1901 by Tad Dorgan, a sports cartoonist, who was attending a baseball game at the famed Polo Grounds in New York. That day, the concession vendors were selling hot dachshund sausages in rolls while yelling, "Get your dachshund sausages while they're red hot!" Dorgan, perched in the press box, sketched a cartoon depicting the scene, but wasn't sure how to spell "dachshund" so he simply called them "hot dogs."

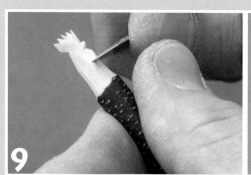

9

To form the beak and wattles, cut two Vs—one to form the bottom of the beak and the top of the wattles, the other to form the bottom of the wattles and the front of the rooster's neck. At this stage, the rooster will have old Dick-Tracy-cartoon-character-type wattles (some of you may remember Dick Tracy's square jaw).

10

Take off the corners and make the wattles look more or less like a half heart, upside down.

Don't Like Hot Dogs?

Cook Something Else on your Newly Whittled Skewer...

Burger on a Stick

- 1 1/2 pounds ground beef
- 1 egg
- 1/4 cup bread crumbs

Mix ground beef, egg, and bread crumbs together. Take a small amount of the mixture, form in the shape of a hot dog, and insert on the end of your skewer. (Make sure it has been cleaned.) Roast over the open fire until the meat is done. Serve on a hot dog bun with ketchup.

Cut a very narrow V-shaped groove to divide the wattles.

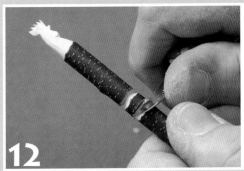 

Cut a couple V-groove rings at the base of the handle of the poker.

Sausage on a Stick

(This is also perfect for breakfast.)

- 1 pre-cooked smoked sausage
- 1 oven-bake, refrigerated breadstick (Pillsbury, etc...)

Spear sausage on your poker. Coil the breadstick dough around the sausage link and pinch the ends. Rotate slowly until bread is browned. Grab the mustard.

Simple Kebab

Slice some vegetables—mushrooms, carrots, tomatoes, peppers—and chunks of meat— pork, sausage, even bacon—and insert randomly on your whittled skewer. Don't make it too heavy; you have to hold it over the embers. Turn occasionally and eat when the meat is crisp and golden brown.

Taper the poker down to a point.

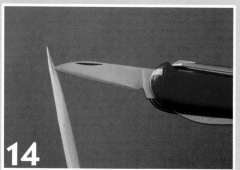

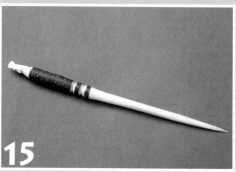

When you do the tapering, make sure you don't have the pith on the very tip of the point. This, of course, will necessitate your making the point of the poker slightly off-center.

Poke away! Just remember, kids, no siblings!

SIZING UP YOUR PROJECT

Try varying the size of your poker to create different tools for different uses. Use a large branch to fashion a spear, a moderately-sized branch for a stake or a spit, smaller pieces for tent pegs, and even smaller sections for toothpicks! If you're really good, try making a needle—cut a slot in the head instead of an eye. If you're using your poker as a kebab skewer, shape it flatter to keep your food pieces from spinning and sliding off when you turn.

To create a rustic spit, make a poker out of a three-foot-long branch. Sharpen the ends of two forked branches; insert them into the ground in your fire pit, making sure the spit will have enough clearance. Center your meat of choice between the forked branches. Spin the spit slowly at regular intervals; it may be several hours until the meat is cooked, depending how large the piece is.

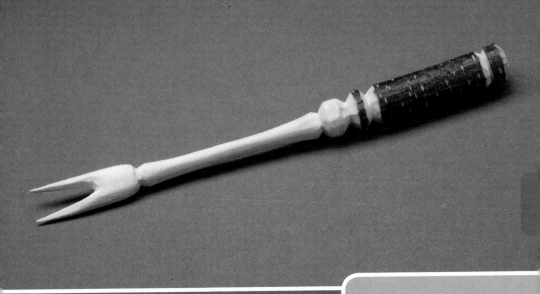

FORK

MATERIALS:

- Knife
- Straight-grained wood of choice
- Sandpaper—a couple of grits on the fine to very fine side (150- and 220-grit would work).
- Polyurethane or other clear finish of choice (optional)
- Pencil, pen, or marker

Forks come in all sizes and can be used to eat, pick up, and roast a number of foods, such as marshmallows and hot dogs. My own versions of forks have three basic components: the handle, the stem, and the fork itself. I've always had just two prongs on my forks, though I'm sure there's no rule against making three or four.

Although there is much debate on the issue, I think whittled forks are better for camping than metal forks, since you won't get "hot hands" from holding a wooden fork over the fire for too long. Also, if you're toasting a harder-to-hold food—anything heavy or slippery—you should use a fork rather than a poker. Forks don't drop their contents as easily.

FORK

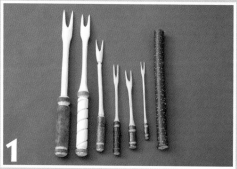

1

Where the variety comes, besides the variety in size itself, is mostly in the handle and stem.

2

Here's our starting blank. The little knot won't be a problem because it is going to disappear in the V-groove ring at the base of the handle.

3

Cut a V-groove to form the handle.

4

Flatten the branch from both sides. Be sure not to take too much off. You want the stem to be thick enough to be strong when it is rounded later on.

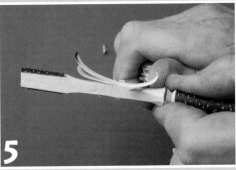

5 Cutting from both ends (toward the center), form the stem of the fork. You'll leave a little wide "paddle" at the end. Round the stem.

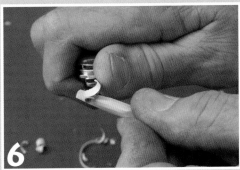

6 Remove the bark from the edges of the "paddle" and taper it to a fairly sharp screwdriver point.

Ultimate Peanut Butter S'mores

Camping just isn't camping without s'mores, and what better way to roast the marshmallows than with an elongated version of this fork? For a change from the garden-variety s'more, try this recipe using peanut butter or a slice of banana. Or instead of using plain old (delicious) chocolate, substitute a peppermint patty. If you want to bring fewer ingredients to the campgrounds, fudge stripe cookies will serve admirably as both chocolate and cookie.

Ingredients:
- Graham crackers
- Chocolate bar
- Marshmallow
- Peanut butter
- Banana (optional)

Place piece of chocolate on graham cracker. Spread with peanut butter. Top with marshmallow. Top with second graham cracker. Wrap in tin foil and let all the flavors melt together.

Add a slice of banana for a super, ultimate version.

Little Tip: To keep matches dry, dip them in wax or nail polish. Use as normal.

FORK

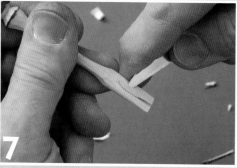 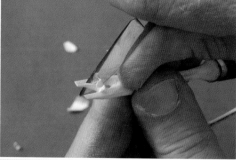

7 Form the two prongs by taking out the V-shaped wedge between them. Note the direction of the cuts. They're always going toward the tips of the prongs—in other words, from the point of the V toward the wide part. This isn't hard to do if you use just the tip of your knife blade.

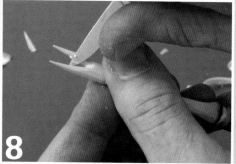

8 Fine-tune the prongs.

HISTORY OF MARSHMALLOW

Marshmallows originated in ancient Egypt where they were made from honey and the sap of the marsh mallow plant's root. Marsh mallow grows in salt marshes and near large bodies of water. Since the 1800s, marshmallows are no longer created with the marsh mallow plant; rather, they are made with gelatin, sugar, and flavoring.

9 Add just a little more decoration between the handle and the stem.

10

And add a little bit more decoration between the prongs and the stem.

ANOTHER GREAT RECIPE:

The Banana Boat

- 1 banana
- Chocolate chips
- Mini-marshmallows
- Tin foil

Pull back one peel of the banana skin—keep attached. Cut a wedge-shaped section the length of the banana. Fill the hollow with mini-marshmallows and chocolate chips. Replace the peel over the mixture. Wrap in tin foil. Insert your fork and cook over fire until the chocolate chips have melted.

FORK

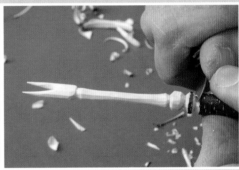

11

Why not...Let's go ahead and give the handle a little more pizzazz, too!

BUILDING A FIRE

If you're camping, a fire is an essential ingredient to making s'mores. Here are two common arrangements for an effective campfire.

Tepee: This arrangement works well for both wet and dry wood. Simply place the wood in a tepee or cone shape. Ignite the wood in the center.

Log Cabin: Start with two logs or branches that are parallel to each other. Place another set of logs on top of and perpendicular to the first layer. Continue to add more layers, each perpendicular to the last. Place tinder and kindling underneath. Light the fire at the bottom of the log cabin.

FORK

12

If you want to clean out and harden the little V-groove rings, you can do so with a little homemade wooden wedge tool.

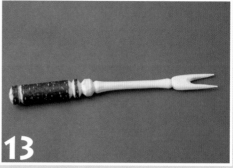

13

Ready to attack your favorite food!

METHODS OF STARTING A FIRE WITHOUT MATCHES

Convex lens: Be sure that you have lots of sun for this method. Position the lens so that the sun's rays focus on the tinder. Once the tinder starts to smolder, fan or blow the tinder until it ignites.

Battery: You'll need a wire or steel wool and a battery with two terminals for this method. If you have steel wool, connect the steel wool to both ends of the battery. Place the tinder in the middle of the steel wool. The sparks should ignite the tinder.

   If you have wire, attach a wire to each terminal. Position yourself close to the tinder and touch the ends of the wires together. The sparks from the wires should ignite the tinder.

Flint and Steel: Strike a hard, sharp rock with a piece of carbon steel. Do not use stainless steel because it will not give you enough of a spark. Once the spark reaches the tinder, blow or fan the tinder until it catches fire.

Bow and Drill: For this method, you'll need a piece of wood that can be easily bent, a hardwood stick (drill), a softwood board, a rock or weight, and a string (a shoestring works well). First make a V-shaped cut in the softwood board. Place tinder under the cut in the board. Make a bow by tying the string to the easily bent piece of wood. Brace the board with your foot and put the string over the drill. Position the drill in the V-shaped cut. Place a rock or some other type of weight on top of the drill for added pressure and hold it in place with one hand. Push down on the drill and move the bow back and forth to spin the drill. The friction created by the drill will grind the tinder and create a spark. Gently blow or fan the spark until the tinder catches fire.

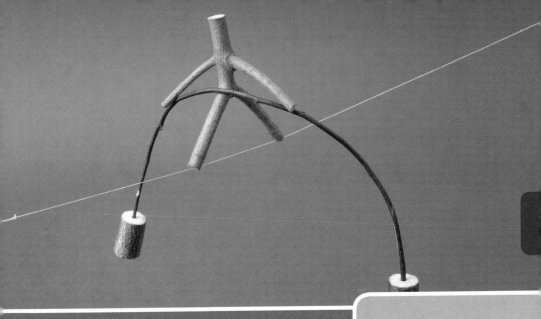

STICK FIGURES

MATERIALS:

- Knife
- Straight-grained wood of choice
- Sandpaper—a couple of grits on the fine to very fine side (150- and 220-grit would work).
- Pencil, pen, or marker
- Dental floss

Over the past four or five decades, as I've hiked through woods or rummaged through branch piles of one description and origin or another, I've stumbled on an amazing variety of almost-already-carved stick figures. Every natural stick figure (at least the "human" type) has a head, a trunk, two arms, and two legs. The position these have grown in determines what the character is doing.

Over the years I've come across some good ones: a discus thrower, a shortstop fielding a hot grounder, a runner carrying the Olympic torch, a gymnast performing a floor exercise move, a soccer player making a perfect trap of the ball, and more.

To some of the basic formations, I've done practically nothing. They've remained in the basic condition in which I found them. Others I've tweaked a little with my pocketknife and some kind of pen or marker. In the following series of photos, we'll create a tightrope walker and look at some of my collection—some hardly touched, others worked on just a bit.

Once you develop an instinct for stick figures, you almost don't have to look for them. They just about jump out at you! You might even want to develop a stick figure collection. See how many different characters you can find.

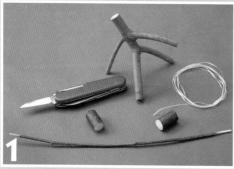

1

With this little maple branch, some dental floss (that's all we could lay our hands on at the photo studio!), and a few more little pieces, let's go for a tightrope walker.

2

Make holes in one end of each of the two little fat "logs."

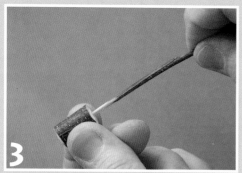

3

Sharpening both ends of the long, thin twig to sharp points, stick them into the holes in the little log weights.

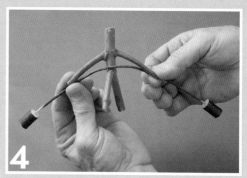

4

See, this is what we're aiming for!

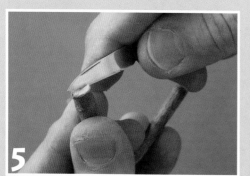

5

Notch a little groove in the bottom of each of the little man's feet. There's no safety net, and you definitely don't want him to slip off the "tightfloss"!

KNOW YOUR KNOTS

Whether your camping or just whittling away, a good grasp of some basic knots will help you on your way. Below are three common types.

Bowline: Can be used whenever a fixed loop is needed at the end of a rope. Great for backpacking and rockclimbing; also useful to hang and hoist objects.

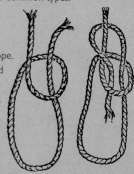

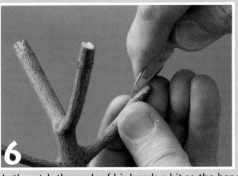

6 Let's notch the ends of his hands a bit so the bar won't slip.

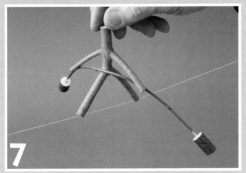

7 We're testing the tightrope walker's position and balance. Oops! We didn't make his balancing rod long enough to create the correct center of gravity.

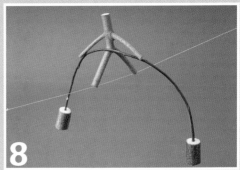

8 Now the bar is long enough and has the proper arc, and our little performer is ready to do his act!

Clove Hitch: The best way to tie a rope to a post or ring. Great for tent pegs and securing an animal to a fence. Also the ideal knot to use when lashing objects together.

Square: Used to tie two lines together.

STICK FIGURES

These are just a few of the stick figures that I have found. Keep your eyes open. There are all kinds of little people and "critters" out there!

STICK FIGURES

First balanced on his left leg and then on his right, this could be either a figure skater or a gymnast doing his floor exercise routine.

Here's a basic "blank" stick figure, one that can be worked on as desired. The wood is maple.

Having been born in Brazil and having played a fair amount of soccer in my lifetime, I especially appreciated this find. He's doing a perfect ball "trap."

An orange branch from a bulldozed Florida orange grove is my discus thrower.

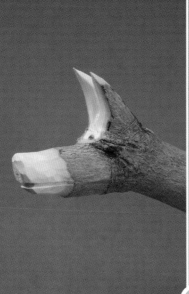

TOPPERS

There are all kinds of animal heads that can emerge from a forked branch and can be used to top canes, walking sticks, or anything else you choose. I'll suggest just three: horse, dog, and goat. What we'll be doing here is just the head and a rather extended neck—you could even drill into the neck and insert a ballpoint pen refill or a pencil lead. If you want to get into the bodies of these animals (caricatures that they are), it's not too hard to combine six more little branch parts of varying sizes: the main body, four legs, and a tail.

MATERIALS:
- Knife
- 3 forked branches of choice
- Sandpaper—a couple of grits on the fine to very fine side (150- and 220-grit would work).
- Polyurethane or other clear finish of choice (optional)
- Pencil, pen, or marker
- Acrylic paints of choice (optional)

HORSE'S HEAD

Here's a horse head I carved many years ago and a blank branch that will become another one. Notice that both of the forks from the base branch are about the same thickness.

It's not necessary to sketch the outline of the figure you're carving, but drawing the profile can be helpful.

Cutting from both the front and back of the head, shape the side profile of the horse's ears.

Round the horse's muzzle.

Make a little V-cut on the front and another on each side to form the mouth.

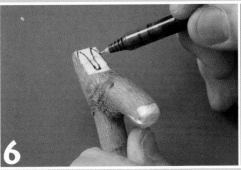

6 Draw the ears and cut them out. This process is similar to the one you use in making the prongs of the fork.

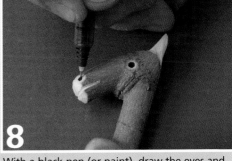

7 Very carefully cut out the bark for the eyes, using small circular strokes. Clean up the eyes by lightly scraping with the point of your knife blade.

8 With a black pen (or paint), draw the eyes and nostrils, and make the mouth stand out more.

9 Finished!

COMMON TYPES OF TRACKS

Deer: Notice the two-part hoof.

Canine and feline: These prints have four toes on both the front and rear feet. Canines that are not domesticated often show claw marks.

Rabbits: Notice the small front feet and large rear feet.

Rodents: Have four toes in front and five in back.

Raccoons: Note that these have five toes on both the front and the rear feet.

1

2

Sketch the profile.

DOG'S HEAD

A previously whittled and a future dog head. The main branch and the lower fork are roughly the same size; the upper fork, for the ears, can be slightly smaller.

3

Shape the profile of the ears.

4

Whittle the dog's muzzle.

5 Draw and cut out a V to separate the ears. Note the directions of these cuts: from the base of the ears toward the points.

6 Draw the eyes and make thin V-cuts to form the mouth.

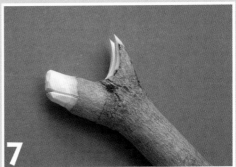

7 The dog would be easy to make into a wolf. You can modify him any way you'd like.

GAIT PATTERNS

Now that you've whittled a few animals, maybe you'd like to look for the real thing. Tracks tell us where animals have been and who they are. Both a footprint itself and the pattern in which the footprints are left tell us about the type of animal that left the tracks. The following categories give some general guidelines for identifying animal tracks.

Animals that Walk in a Diagonal Pattern: These animals move their left front and right back feet together and then their right front and left back feet together, and so on. Dogs, cats, and horses, for example, all move in this manner.

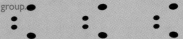

Animals that Hop: Animals in this group jump with their back feet then land with their front feet. Rabbits are a prime example of this group.

Animals that Waddle: Waddlers move their right front and right rear feet together then their left front and left rear feet together, and so on. Raccoons leave tracks in this pattern.

Animals that Bound: These animals move both front feet together and then both back feet together. Otters have this type of gait.

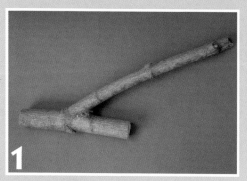

Goat's Head

Here's our starting piece.

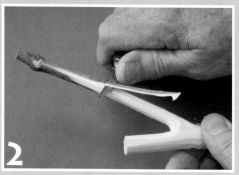

For the goat we'll de-bark the whole branch.

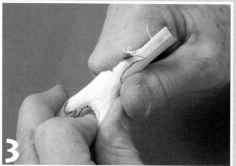

Sketch the side profile of the goat's head. Don't forget the horns and goatee! Next, carve the profile of the horns. Be careful with the grain as you make those curved strokes.

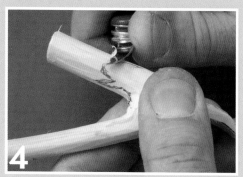

Taper the nose piece and cut off the excess length.

Sketch the front profile of the nose and horns. Shape the nose and goatee.

You may want to take a little wood out from the goat's neck area.

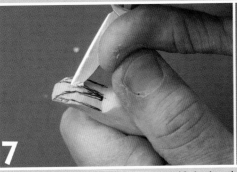

7

Cut out the horns, rounding them and bringing them to a point. Again, careful with the grain!

8

Notch out the mouth and fine-tune the goatee.

9

Our progress so far.

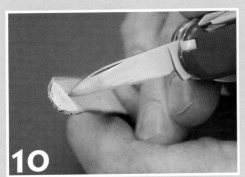

10

Take another branch and flatten it from one side, removing the wood to just past the pith.

11

Draw and cut out two ears.

Little Tip: Use deck water sealant to waterproof your tent, poncho, etc.

12 Shape the ears.

13 Position the ears on the head. With the point of your blade, make holes on each side of the head. Press the ears into the holes to test their position.

14 Remove the ears and sand the head smooth.

15 Having the ears in place helps locate the position of the eyes. Draw them in. Darken the mouth groove and draw the nostrils while you're at it.

16 Permanent ears at last! Just a little wood glue in the holes will hold the goat's ears in place.

17 Here's the finished goat head.

DUCK

MATERIALS:
- Knife
- Forked branch of choice
- Sandpaper—a couple of grits on the fine to very fine side (150- and 220-grit would work).
- Polyurethane or other clear finish of choice (optional)
- Pencil, pen, or marker
- Acrylic paints of choice (optional)

To the best of my recollection, in my over 35 years of branch carving, besides the little cartoonish duck illustrated in the following photos, I've had the chance to carve very few ducks, and those were even more of a caricature than this one. Even though I don't carve ducks very often, the first little guy I carved was one of the most popular pieces in my collection of carvings. Unfortunately, it got lost in one of my case-falling-over accidents almost 20 years ago, having long ago turned into mulch in the grass of South Jersey.

Though the one I'm carving here is somewhat of a caricature, feel free to make yours as realistic or as cartoonish as you like. You can also paint your duck in a variety of colors to match your favorite species.

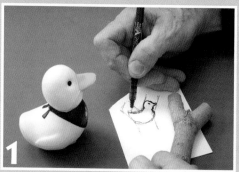

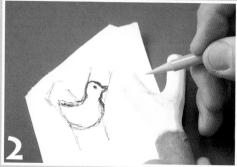

Choose a fork that has both top parts of the Y with close to the same diameter. Sketch the duck you're aiming for.

De-bark the duck portion of the branch and sketch a few lines on the wood.

Begin by rounding the head.

DEALING WITH SNAKES

If you're a duck hunter, you know that you need good snake boots before you get out in the blind. Nobody wants to be snake bait—not even duck whittlers! These venomous critters can be downright nasty, so here's some advice on how to deal with them.

What to do if you're bitten by a snake:

- Clean the infected area with soap and water.
- Position the bitten area so that it is immobile and below the heart.
- Seek medical attention immediately. People can have adverse reactions to both poisonous and nonpoisonous snakebites.

- If you are more than 30 minutes from a medical care facility, wrap a bandage two to four inches above the bite to help slow the venom. The bandage should not be so tight that it cuts off circulation.
- Consider using suction to help remove venom from the wound.

What not to do:

- Do not ice the wound.
- Do not use a tourniquet.
- Do not cut into the bitten area.

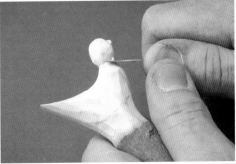

4 Finish shaping the head and taper the tail branch.

5 Round the tail a bit and cut in from the front and back to round the bottom of the duck's body.

6 Sand the whole duck, if you want a smooth finish. If you'd rather have the cut marks showing, just leave the little guy as he is.

TYPES OF POISONOUS SNAKES COMMON IN THE U.S.

- Rattlesnakes
- Copperheads
- Cottonmouths (water moccasins)
- Coral snakes

Some nonpoisonous snakes, such as the scarlet king snake, mimic the bright red, yellow, and black colors of the coral snake. This potential confusion emphasizes the importance of seeking care for any snakebite, regardless of the nature of the snake.

Ways to Avoid Snakes and Snakebites

- Stay away. Don't try to kill or get too close to a snake. Keep at least six feet between you and the snake.
- Wear thick boots, long pants, and long-sleeved shirts in areas where snakes are common.
- Don't reach or step where you can't see.
- Be aware. Always look around you as you are hiking or climbing and be on the lookout for snakes.

7

The duck at this point.

8

Paint the beak yellow. I usually use an acrylic paint.

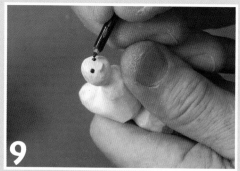

9

Paint the eyes black.

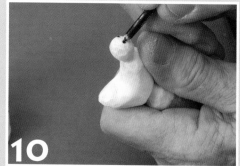

10

There are several directions you can go from here: 1) Cut him (or her—it could be either) off and let him swim; 2) Work on some little legs and feet and let him stand; 3) Cut him off and let him settle in a nest; 4) Leave him on the post trying to be a rooster (like the duck in the movie *Babe*).

EVERYTHING'S DUCKY

Everyone loves feeding the ducks; however, feeding them often makes them tame and dependant on humans. Bread especially isn't good for ducks; it fills them up without giving the vital nutrition necessary for migration and reproduction. If you want to feed your feathered friends, throw foods like barley, corn, and wheat.

SONGBIRD

MATERIALS:
- Knife
- Forked branch of choice
- Sandpaper—a couple of grits on the fine to very fine side (150- and 220-grit would work).
- Polyurethane or other clear finish of choice (optional)
- Pencil, pen, or marker
- Acrylic paints of choice (optional)

A number of years ago, I took one of my neighbor's kids to an Orioles baseball game at the beautiful Camden Yards stadium in Baltimore. As usual I "just happened to have" a few little twigs along for the ride. Sometime during our stay out in the left field corner of the stands, I started to whittle a miniature Baltimore oriole, first using the big oriole on the scoreboard as a pattern and then borrowing my little neighbor's Orioles baseball cap. The little oriole came out pretty well! I think the fans sitting directly behind us got as big a charge out of the oriole carving as they did out of the baseball game.

There are zillions of species of songbirds, and I can't really tell you which one we're doing here. Anyway, let's call this a "generic songbird." For those of you who are into all of the distinctions and subtle nuances of the countless variety of birds, experiment and make the necessary adaptations, both in the carving itself as well as in the painting and finishing.

1

Here's a bird (looking down, in this case) and an appropriate blank fork.

2

Remove the bark from the entire fork.

3

Sketch the side profile of the bird.

4

Flatten the top and the bottom of the tail.

5

Shape the side profile of the head.

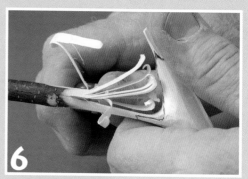

6

Taper the leg branch.

7 Cut off the excess length from the beak branch and taper the tail a bit more.

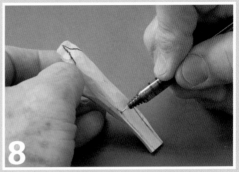

8 Draw the top view of the head and beak and tail.

9 Carve the head and sharpen the beak.

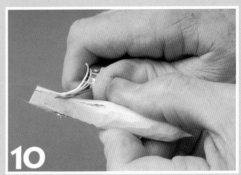

10 Carve the tail.

11 Draw lines for rounding the underside of the body a bit more.

12 The body a bit more rounded with the legs a little more pronounced.

13 Draw the two legs.

14 Very carefully cut out the wedge between the legs. Again, where you go from this point is totally up to you! Fine-tune the details, and have fun painting and mounting.

CAMPFIRE SINGING

After whittling your songbird, why not join it in some campfire singing?

On Top of Old Smoky

On top of old Smoky, all covered with snow,
I lost my true lover from courting too slow.

Now, courting is pleasure and parting is grief,
And a false-hearted lover is worse than a thief.

For a thief will just rob you and take what you have,
But a false-hearted lover will lead you to the grave.

And the grave will decay you and turn you to dust;
Not one boy in a hundred a poor girl can trust.

They'll hug you and kiss you and tell you more lies,
Than cross ties on a railroad or stars in the skies.

So, come all you young maidens and listen to me,
Never place your affection on a green willow tree.

For the leaves they will whither, and the roots
they will die,
You'll all be forsaken and never know why.

Oh! Susanna

I come from Alabama with my banjo on my knee,
I'm going to Louisiana, my true love for to see.
It rained all night the day I left, the weather it was dry
The sun so hot I froze to death, Susanna, don't you cry.

Chorus

Oh! Susanna, Oh don't you cry for me,
For I come from Alabama with my banjo on my knee.

I had a dream the other night, when everything
was still;
I thought I saw Susanna dear, a coming down the hill.
A buckwheat cake was in her mouth, a tear was in
her eye,
Says I, I'm coming from the south, Susanna, don't
you cry.

I soon will be in New Orleans, and then I'll look
around,
And when I find Susanna, I'll fall upon the ground.
But if I do not find her, then I will surely die,
And when I'm dead and buried, Oh, Susanna,
don't you cry.

JUMPING FISH

MATERIALS:

- Knife
- Forked branch of choice
- Sandpaper—a couple of grits on the fine to very fine side (150- and 220-grit would work).
- Pencil, pen, or marker

Fish of all kinds are another specialty of many woodcarvers. When I attend carving shows, I'm totally amazed at the incredible lifelikeness and detail of the fish I see. If we dropped some of these carvings in a large aquarium, we'd never know we weren't observing live fish! The fish that follows is definitely not intended to fall into the same category as the earlier-mentioned works of art. However, I think you'll enjoy carving it. I know I did.

For this project, I'm indebted to fellow branch carver Mike Shatt of Milford, Pennsylvania. Quite a few years back, I met Mike and introduced him to the concept of carving twigs and branches. Several years ago, Mike sent me a few photos of pieces he had carved. Among them were several of fish jumping out of water, complete with splash! Based on his idea, I tried similar fish myself. If you don't have a branch with another little branch growing from the side to make the fish's dorsal fin, you can use a separate branch for the dorsal fin.

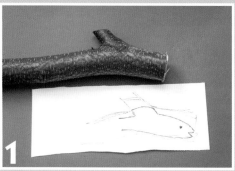

1 If you can, start with a blank branch that has better built-in potential for a good dorsal fin. Start by making a little sketch.

2 Remove all of the bark from the entire branch.

3 Sketch the outline of the fish.

4 Remove wood from outside the lines.

BEST BAITS

Nice fish! However, if you're hungry, you might not want to eat it. Here are some tips to help you catch a non-wooden version.

The best baits for fishing depend a great deal on the location and the type of fish you want to catch. The following chart shows some common baits and the category of fish they're used to catch. Check any fishing regulations before you fish to make sure the bait you choose is legal for the location where you are fishing.

Bait	Type of Environment	Fish Commonly Caught
Worms	freshwater	bass, catfish, panfish
Leeches	freshwater	bass
Minnows	freshwater	gamefish
Crayfish	freshwater	trout, bass, catfish
Crickets	freshwater	trout, panfish
Grasshoppers	freshwater	trout, panfish
Eels	saltwater	bass
Crabs	saltwater	redfish, snapper, grouper
Shrimp	saltwater	gamefish
Squid	saltwater	mackerel
Pieces of fish	saltwater	tuna

5 Taper the dorsal fin branch.

6 Draw the top of the dorsal fin and finish shaping it.

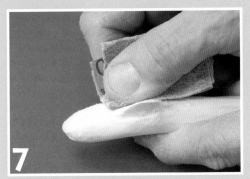

7 Sand the whole fish smooth.

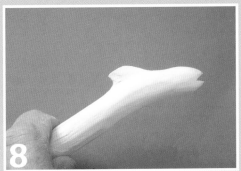

8 Here's where we stand now.

How to Bait a Hook

Worms: Thread the hook through the worm in several places.

Leeches: Hook them through the sucker.

Minnows: Thread the hook through both the top and bottom lip, through the tail, or through the back.

Crayfish: Put the hook through the tail.

Insects: Thread the hook through the abdomen.

Eels: Put the hook through the eyes or lips.

Crabs: Cut into sections and hook the sections.

Shrimp: Can be alive or dead. Place the hook through the tail or use cut-up pieces of shrimp for bait.

Squid: Place the hook through the head.

Pieces of fish: Be sure to hook through the skin.

9

With the tip of your small blade, drawcut little shavings all the way around the fish. These little shavings and curls will constitute the upward-splashing water.

10

Make four little forward cuts to add the fish's other little fins. What you'll be doing is just lifting a little shaving to serve as a fin.

11

Once again, you take it from here! One option is to cut the wood just below the splash and mount it on a cross-grained slice of wood with the growth rings clearly visible. The rings sort of give the effect of ripples radiating out from the splash. The kind of fish you carve will, of course, determine more precise shaping and finishing.

TIPS FOR COOKING TROUT

- Fry trout at 325°F or higher.
- Fresh trout should be used within about two days.
- Don't place trout closer than four inches from the heat source when broiling.
- For the most part, trout is done when it flakes easily with a fork.

SIMPLE TROUT RECIPE

Ingredients:

- 1 fresh trout
- 2 slices bacon
- 1 large onion, chopped
- 1 tablespoon butter
- Salt and pepper

Once the fish is cleaned and gutted, rinse it off and pat it dry. Butter the insides and add salt and pepper (or other seasonings) as desired, then stuff with onion. Butter the outside of the fish as well; then wrap it in two slices of bacon. Wrap the fish in aluminum foil and place it on a grill or directly on the coals. Cook for approximately 10 minutes.

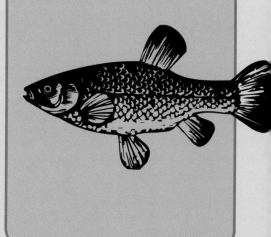

FLOWER

MATERIALS:
- Knife
- Straight-grained wood of choice
- Sandpaper—a couple of grits on the fine to very fine side (150- and 220- grit would work).
- Polyurethane or other clear finish of choice (optional)
- Pencil, pen, or marker
- Oil paints of choice or acrylic paints of choice and CA glue (optional)

Over the years, I've whittled thousands of little flowers, the majority just given to folks along the way. I used to throw little scraps away until I discovered that just about every single one of them could be turned into a flower, complete with petals, stem, and leaves.

Carving this type of flower is really not that uncommon. Many people do it. I'll just share my own take on a quick and fun little project, one that can be expanded upon and applied very widely.

Most of the flowers of this type that I've seen are quite a bit larger than the ones I make. Usually the flower itself is made and cut off; then, a stem of some kind is inserted in a little hole that is drilled in the base of the flower. My own flowers are all made from one continuous piece of wood, usually a thin, close-grained twig or branch. The branches I use are relatively straight, don't have many knots, and generally are from 1/16 inch to 1/4 inch in diameter. Because moisture really affects the petals in this project, be sure to find wood that is between freshly cut and completely dry. A freshly cut branch that is de-barked will dry nicely in a relatively short time, maybe even in a few hours.

FLOWER

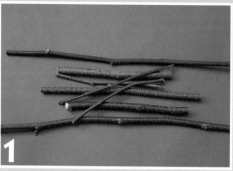

1

Eight little starting blanks. I'm guessing that these branches could result in 18 to 20 flowers, complete with stems and leaves.

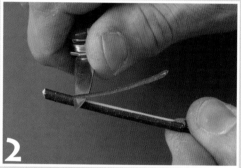

2

Using long, straight strokes, remove the bark from the branch. (Some carvers prefer to leave the bark on the branch in order to give the outside ring of petals a different look. If you decide to do this, make sure the wood you're using has tight bark that won't just fall off after the flower dries out.)

LEAVES OF THREE, LET IT BE!

The best way to avoid the itch during your camping trip is to learn how to identify poisonous plants. Poison ivy and oak both have clusters of three leaves; ivy has the teardrop-shaped leaves we all know, while oak has distinctly oak-shaped leaves. Look for alternating groups of leaves (not directly across from each other on the vines). Poison sumac can have 7 to 13 leaves on each stem; also, look for smooth leaf edges and white hanging berries. Sumac also prefers marshy soil; stay away from swamps and you'll avoid it. Add "Berries white, run in fright!" to the old adage and you'll be fully aware of the most common poisonous plants around you. According to the American Academy of Dermatology, approximately 85 percent of the population will develop an allergic reaction if exposed to poison ivy, oak, or sumac. If you do come in contact with one of these plants, follow these directions:

1. Cleanse skin with rubbing alcohol.

2. Wash with water.

3. Take a shower with soap and water. (Note: Do not use soap prior to this step to avoid transferring the poison to the soap.)

4. Wash shoes, clothing, or any other items that have been exposed with rubbing alcohol and water. Wear gloves to avoid additional exposure.

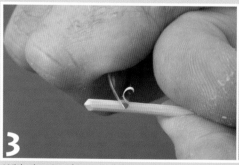

3

With the tip of your small blade, carve and twist down the first layer of petals, cutting all the way around the branch, always cutting down to the same depth.

4

Carve down another layer or two. Try to position the second layer of petals between the petals of the previously carved layer.

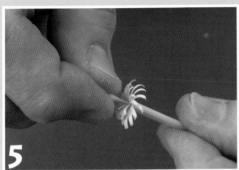 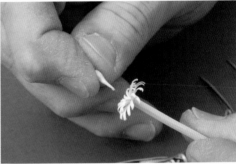

5

Twist out the little central core that's left in the middle.

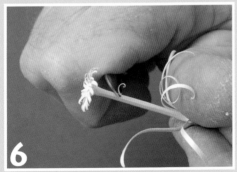

6

Taper down the stem, bringing it into better proportion in relation to the size of the flower. (Of course you can always leave the stem thick. Then you have a little palm tree!)

AVOIDING POISONOUS PLANTS

As a general rule of thumb, avoid plants with any of the following characteristics:

- Milky sap.
- Beans, bulbs, or seeds in pods.
- A bitter or soapy taste.
- Spines, fine hairs, or thorns.
- Foliage similar to dill, carrot, parsnip, or parsley.
- The smell of almond in woody parts or leaves.
- Groupings of three leaves.

Little Fact: Washington's Beacon Rock State Park is known for its unique rock structures. **67**

7

Carve down a couple more little shavings to serve as the leaves.

8

"Pick" the flower at the bottom of the stem. Feel free to move the petals around a bit and position them where you want. They're really very sturdy and forgiving. Now the flower is ready for finishing: painting, mounting, "planting," and whatever else you choose. I've found that chunks of bark or thick mulch serve nicely as natural bases.

TREE

MATERIALS:

- Knife
- Straight-grained wood of choice
- Sandpaper—a couple of grits on the fine to very fine side (150- and 220-grit would work).
- Pencil, pen, or marker
- CA glue

Though this project may take some concentration, it's a lot of fun, and many people really like whittling this type of tree. Every single one I've ever made to sell has found a buyer. While this miniature tree is in some respects similar to those from Europe that you may have seen, in other ways it's quite different. For one, the branches come down in a spiral, rather than having a succession of layers of branches that each merge at the same level on the trunk. For this tree, you really do need a straight branch that has no knots at all anywhere along the entire tree portion.

1

With long, straight strokes remove all of the bark. (Short, choppy strokes will make for uneven, hard-to-control branch cutting.)

2

Taper the point of the branch—sort of like sharpening a pencil the old-fashioned way.

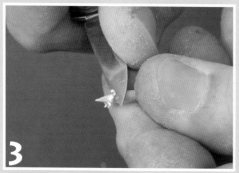

3

With the thumb of the hand that's holding the blade braced against the finger(s) of the hand that's holding the branch, make very small, controlled shaving cuts toward the point of the stick.

TWELVE OF THE MOST POPULAR NATIONAL PARKS (in alphabetical order)

A tree is a good carving project, but the real thing is even better! Visit these parks for a beautiful display of non-whittled trees and other beautiful natural creations. **If you want to whittle at state or national parks, be sure to check their regulations regarding using any wood within their borders before you carve.**

- Acadia National Park, Maine
- Bryce Canyon National Park, Utah
- Death Valley National Park, California
- Denali National Park, Alaska
- Everglades National Park, Florida
- Glacier Bay National Park and Preserve, Alaska
- Grand Canyon National Park, Arizona
- Grand Teton National Park, Wyoming
- Great Smoky Mountains National Park, Tennessee and North Carolina
- Rocky Mountain National Park, Colorado
- Yellowstone National Park, Wyoming
- Yosemite National Park, California

DON'T FEED THE BEARS!

In national parks, bears that have acquired a taste for human food can be very dangerous. For this reason, it is of the utmost importance that visitors don't feed any of the wildlife in the parks. In 1998 in Yosemite National Park, bears broke into over 1,300 parked vehicles and caused over $630,000 in damage. The number of bear break-ins dropped to 318 in 1999 because of the park rangers' work to educate visitors.

Remember that feeding the bears is bad for humans and bad for the bears. When bears become dangerous in their attempts to get human food, they must often be put to death or be relocated. Having human food available also disrupts bears' natural instincts.

4

Each little branch will be the slightest bit longer than the preceding one.

5

Remember, always keep your blade-holding thumb braced against at least the forefinger of your wood-holding hand. If you don't use this steadying and braking system and instead try to "freehand" the cut, there's a good chance that you'll lose control and slice off several of the previously made branches! I usually tend to finish my last few branches by making them a bit shorter as I wind down to the end.

6

Reinforce the bases of the branches with a bit of CA glue. The glue soaks in and kind of petrifies them.

7

Chop down the tree.

Little Fact: Visit Monahans Sandhills State Park in western Texas to sled on the sand dunes.

TREE

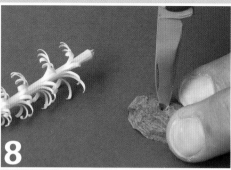

8

Make a planting hole in a little bark base.

9

Glue the tree in place, checking it from all angles to make sure it's standing straight.

10

Three trees done! Now carve the tree ornaments and lights!

METHODS OF KEEPING ANIMALS FROM GETTING TO YOUR FOOD

Whenever you are camping, you'll want to consider where you will store your food so that wild animals do not visit your camp in search of food. Keep the following guidelines in mind, and be sure to supplement them with advice from rangers or other authorities in your camping area.

- Never leave your food, even if it's still in your pack, unattended.

- Empty your pack overnight, and leave all pockets and compartments open. This way, nocturnal visitors can snoop around without being tempted to gnaw at or shred your gear to see what's inside.

- Cook meals and store food at least 100 feet away from your sleeping area. Keep food in airtight containers to help contain the smell. Anything with a heavy aroma—powder, ointment, toothpaste, sunscreen, bug spray, lotion—should also be stored with your food, as animals are drawn to any exotic smells. Keep the stash downwind of your site, if possible.

- Use bear boxes, bear wires, or bear poles if available.

- Alternate your hiding place; don't use the same place every time. Animals are creatures of habit and will come back to the same places in search of food. You'll also want to avoid using the same tree other campers have already used.

- Keep a clean camp. The best way to prevent animals from visiting your campsite is to not give them any incentives to come or to stay.

- Never feed a wild animal.

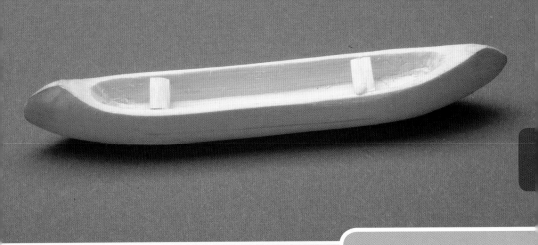

Canoe

Materials:
- Knife
- Straight-grained wood of choice
- Sandpaper—a couple of grits on the fine to very fine side (150- and 220-grit would work).
- Polyurethane or other clear finish of choice (optional)
- Pencil, pen, or marker
- Chisel or screwdriver
- CA glue

My love for canoes came very honestly. My Brooklyn, New York-born dad and Hays, Kansas-born mom raised me in some of the more primitive parts of Brazil and Peru. I learned to swim very close to alligators and piranhas, and I spent many happy hours up in trees and in a variety of planes, motorboats, and dugout canoes. Tom Sawyer and Huck Finn really didn't have much on us kids that swam and canoed the Ucayali River and traveled on river launches that had the awful smell of hundreds and hundreds of salted alligator hides!

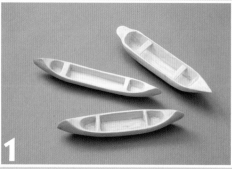

1

The little canoe at the top is similar to the dugouts I paddled around in as a kid on the Ucayali River in the eastern jungles of Peru back in the early 1950s. The two lower canoes are shaped more or less like the average North American canoe.

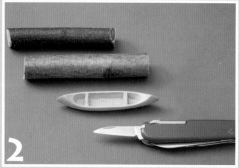

2

We're going to use the thicker of these two branches and make a canoe shaped like the one between the branch and the pocketknife.

3

Remove all of the bark from the branch.

4

Draw the side profile of the canoe.

5 Begin shaping the canoe by flattening the bottom and bringing the bottom up at the ends.

6 Sketch the canoe's profile from a top view.

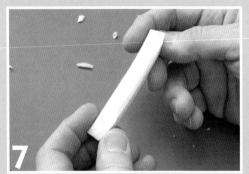

7 Taper the two ends to a point. Of course, now you've cut off the side profile lines!

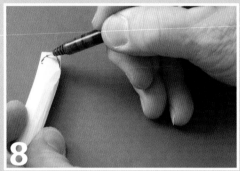

8 Redraw the side profile.

9 Following the lines, carve the two ends of the canoe.

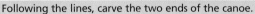

Little Tip: Don't toss that waxed cardboard milk carton! Cut it into pieces and use as kindling. **75**

CANOE

10

Cutting toward center from both ends, shape the top of the main body of the canoe.

11

Here we are so far.

12

Fine-tune the bottom curves, blending them into the points with a nice taper.

WHAT TO BRING FOR CANOE CAMPING

Because canoe camping is a combination of camping and canoeing, you'll need some special equipment for any trips that you may take. The following items are just some things to consider.

- Extra clothes—Since there's a greater danger of getting wet, extra clothing is a must.
- Personal flotation device—Bring at least one per person and a few extras.
- First-aid kit—Always a good idea; be sure to include any special medications or prescriptions as needed.
- Fishing license and equipment—If the place you've chosen allows fishing, don't forget your gear.
- Waterproof clothing—Raingear is a must to help keep you dry.
- Insect repellent—Insects are often more abundant around water, so pack plenty of repellent.
- Paddle and paddling gloves—Bring extras, too.

- Rescue equipment—Should at least include rope and an extra personal flotation device.
- Waterproof maps—Products are available so that you can seal your own maps.
- Bailer or bilge pump—For any emergencies.
- Eyewear retainers for sunglasses or glasses—To prevent them from being lost. Bringing a few extra pairs of glasses is also a good idea.
- Car-top canoe racks—To get your canoe to the site.
- Radio—To keep you informed about weather alerts.
- Clothesline—For drying those wet clothes.
- Camp stove—For those great campfire recipes, especially if fires are prohibited.
- Drinking water—Especially if the river water is not drinkable.
- Water purification tablets or crystals—To purify any river water if necessary.

13

Using fine sandpaper, smooth the whole boat.

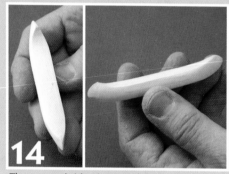

14

The top and side views at this stage.

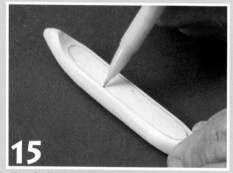

PLANNING A CANOE CAMPING TRIP

Canoe camping is a boatload of fun; just don't try it in one of the canoes you just whittled! This great variation of regular camping can be tricky because of its added element—canoeing. Consider some of the following tips before you head out to the campsite.

- Try packing anything that you want readily accessible in a separate bag. The items will be easy to find when you're ready to head out for a day hike or when you want to head home, and you won't have to dig through any larger bags.

- Make sure you have all gear specific to your canoe together, and waterproof anything that requires it (i.e., maps).

- Of course, you'll want to have all of your camping equipment ready to go as well. Making separate lists for camping items, canoeing items, and other such categories will ensure that you are completely prepared.

- Plan your food and meal needs based on what's available at the site and your personal preference. Foods with little waste and packaging will help to keep your campsite clean. Find out if fires are permitted, and have a back-up method for cooking food just in case.

- Canoe camping requires a generous amount of extra clothes and clothes for all types of weather—layering is often effective. Be sure to pack accordingly. Check out the typical weather in your camping area, and plan for weather 20 degrees in either extreme. Hypothermia can be a danger in cold and rainy weather.

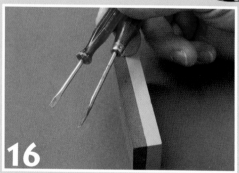

15

Sketch the inside wall.

16

Time out! While there's a lot you're still going to do with your knife blade, there's virtually no way you're going to be able to flatten the bottom of the inside of your canoe without some kind of little chisel. Since I didn't have any little chisels lying around, I made my own from little screwdrivers I had.

17 Using a little stone and a strop, I made a pretty decent chisel. You can see its profile in the photo on the right.

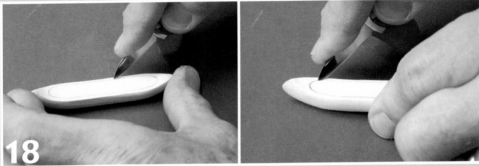

18 Very carefully, with the tip of the knife blade, cut in around the whole outline of the canoe's inside walls. Take it easy and take it slow! You don't want to slice through the wall.

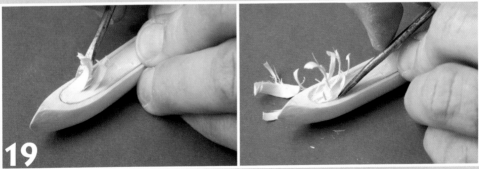

19 Begin hollowing out the inside from both ends, using the chisel.

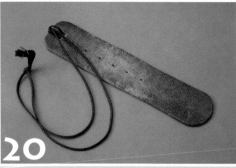

20 If you want to cut toward yourself (and there's a good chance that you will), make a little chest guard with a piece of old leather belt. Now you can make all kinds of little crisscrossed V-cuts.

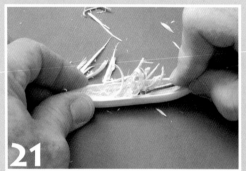

21 With the chisel, clean out all of the little rough stuff.

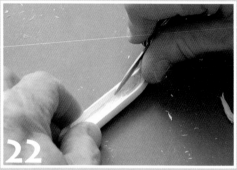

22 Trim the inside walls with your knife blade.

23 Rasp the bottom as smooth as possible with your little chisel.

HOW TO PURIFY RIVER WATER

If, for some reason, you need to use river water for drinking, you'll need to purify it first. The following methods are two of the most common.

- Boil the water—Bringing the water to a full boil kills almost all living organisms, including bacteria, viruses, and parasites. Let the water cool before drinking.
- Treatments—Products, usually in the form of tablets or crystals, are available to treat water without boiling it.

Note: Neither of these methods removes chemical pollutants from water, so if you suspect water is polluted (you can see the pollution or smell it), don't use the water.

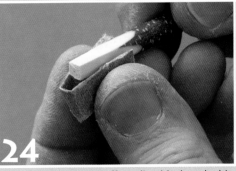

24

Using a little squared-off sanding block and a bit of sandpaper, smooth the inside of the canoe.

25

Thin down a little "board" to make a couple of seats. Insert them and glue them in place.

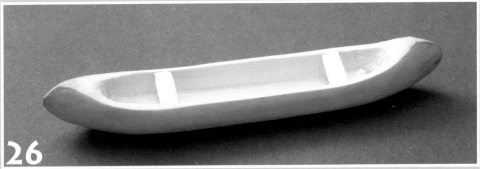

26

Now all you have to do is carve a couple of mini-miniature paddles and put them in the hands of a couple of mini-miniature figures, and they're ready to go...well, downstream, I guess.

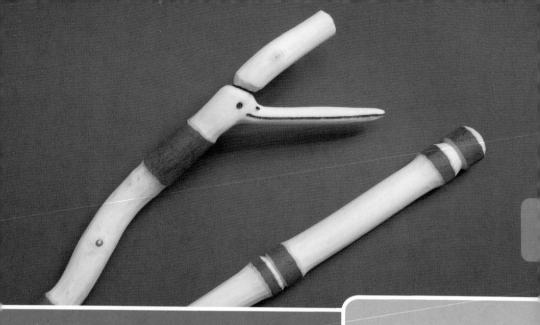

WALKING STICK

MATERIALS:

- Knife
- Straight-grained wood of choice
- Sandpaper—a couple of grits on the fine to very fine side (150- and 220-grit would work).

A number of years ago when the new Sarasota Middle School in Florida was being built, a whole citrus grove was cleared to make room for it. Needless to say, the bulldozers made mountains and mountains of wonderful raw material. (Citrus wood is great for this type of carving. Florida residents, keep your eyes peeled for rising middle schools or whatever!) Out of the piles of fallen trees and branches came a number of things, not the least useful of which was the crutch I made to help me hobble around after a basketball injury. I think it might have been from the same pile of wood that I got the very nice cane that is currently hanging in my shop.

I'm sure there are many volumes that have been written on walking sticks. I definitely don't consider myself even the slightest expert on carving them, and I'm certainly not trying in any way to compete with all the great walking stick literature that's already out there. All I want to do is suggest a couple of simple projects that some folks might enjoy as they hike along some portion of their "journey."

Not too long ago, one of my neighbors topped several of his maple trees. I think all of these particular walking stick blanks came from the huge pile of branches in his backyard. While none of them is perfectly straight (they really don't need to be), they're all thick enough to support a decent amount of weight. Remember, as you choose a branch for your walking stick, pick a species of wood that is hard enough and thick enough to be reliable.

Here are the heads of two walking stick blanks. We'll work on the straight one in my hand.

This stick is about 1 1/8 inches in diameter.

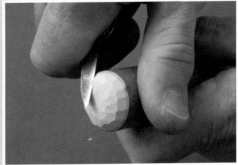

Round the top of the handle. When you're doing the drawing cuts for this part, make sure you keep your thumb lower on the branch so that, when your blade does its follow-through jump after clearing the wood, it doesn't do a little operation on your thumb! Some folks like to use thumb guards or tape. I personally don't. However, I've learned to position my thumb so it's out of the way of speeding and jumping knife blades.

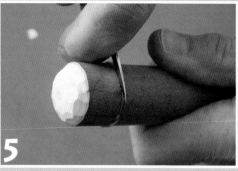
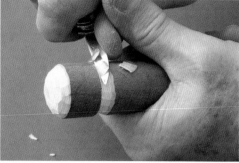

5

By making a wider V-groove ring than you carved in the knife or fork handles, create a knob.

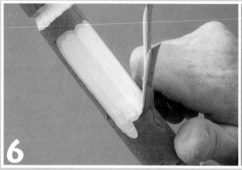

6

Remove the bark around the branch below the knob to form your handgrip.

7

Carve another ring below the handgrip.

Little Tip: Don't chuck that orange peel: Cook eggs in half of an orange peel right in the fire. **83**

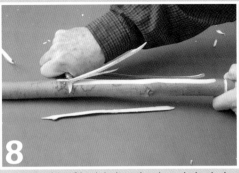
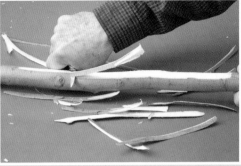

8

Leaving a bit of bark below the ring, de-bark the rest of the walking stick.
(If you do this while the wood is still fresh, it's a lot easier.)

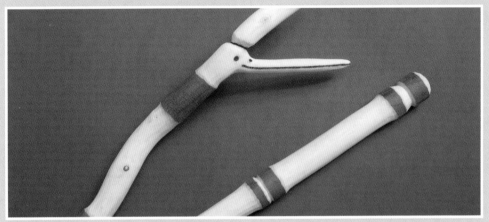

Here are the two handles on the two walking
stick blanks we started out with.

TRAIL SNACKS

Here are some delicious one-handed trail snacks
that will allow you to keep that other hand on your
walking stick!

The Trail Apple

- I apple
- Peanut butter
- Chocolate chips
- Raisins
- Peanuts or mixed nuts

Remove the core of the apple. Stuff with peanut
butter and any or all of the ingredients listed above.
Wrap in plastic wrap and off you go.
A great snack…

GORP

So did GORP derive its name from the acronym
Good **O**ld **R**aisins and **P**eanuts or from **G**ranola
Oats **R**aisins and **P**eanuts? Not a clue…but make
sure you have plenty while out on the trail. To make
your own, simply mix the ingredients listed in a
sealed plastic bag. Or get creative and toss together
any combination of nuts, seeds, raisins, or any other
dried fruit and oats. A few ideas:

Mixed Nut Gorp

- I cup mixed dried roasted nuts
- I cup dried fruit
- I cup M&M's
- I cup roasted sunflower seeds

Cereal Gorp

- I cup cereal (Chex, Cheerios, Kashi)
- I cup peanuts
- I cup M&M's
- I cup raisins

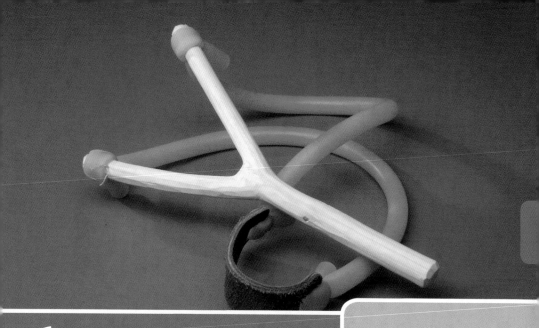

SLINGSHOT

MATERIALS:

- Knife
- Hardwood fork in a reasonably symmetrical Y
- Sandpaper—a couple of grits on the fine to very fine side (150- and 220-grit would work).
- Good-quality surgical tubing
- Leather for the pocket
- Dental floss

As with canoes, my interest in slingshots came very naturally, as it also did with bows and arrows, different kinds of traps, tree houses, and peashooters (except we made little clay balls to shoot in our nice, straight bamboo barrels). Though I'm not proud of all of the things I did as a kid with my many slingshots, I did do a lot of fun and useful things, too—like pick way-out-on-a-limb, impossible-to-reach mangoes!

Of course it was a two-person job. One stood under the huge, beautiful, ripe mango, and the other stood off a ways armed with a nice, hard green guava or palm nut and a good slingshot. The idea, naturally, was not to hit the mango itself. That would bruise it unmercifully. The actual target was the long stem just above the mango. This being clipped by the speeding "bullet," the mango would come straight down, into the hands (hopefully) of the waiting catcher.

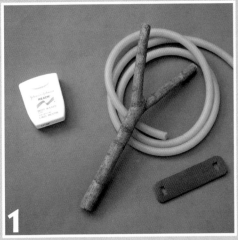

The components for a 2005 Lubkemann adaptation of a 1950s Brazilian slingshot, Mato Grosso style: a hardwood fork in a reasonably symmetrical Y; good-quality surgical tubing (how thick depends on how strong a pull you want); a good piece of leather for the pocket; and dental floss (yes, dental floss!—it can be mint-flavored or plain, and I generally use waxed). At this point, I should confess that, as a kid in the jungle, I used strips of good old genuine rubber inner tubing, worn-out shoe tongues, and string! But I suspect it's impossible to find real rubber inner tubes anymore; leather shoe tongues probably aren't all that easy to come by; and as for substituting dental floss for string, I don't really remember how I started doing that, but it works great! It's very strong and doesn't slip when you're tying it.

Cut the handle branch to a length you feel comfortable with.

Round off the tops of the two top stems of the fork.

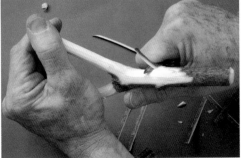

For this particular fork, we'll strip all of the bark off. For some of my slingshot forks, I leave on part of the bark, depending on what I want the final fork to look like.

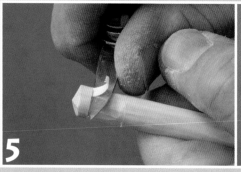

5 Cut a shallow notch around the top of each of the rubber-holding branches.

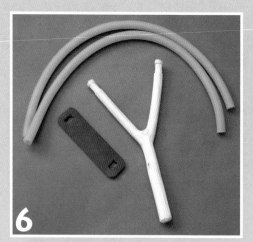

6 Cut the tubing to the length you want, remembering that you're going to fold the ends around the shallow notches in the two top stems and through the holes you've carefully cut in the piece of leather. When you cut the holes in the leather pouch, make sure you cut very carefully so as not to overcut, thus leaving little cuts that can develop into rips or tears in the leather.

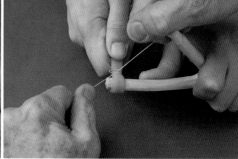

7 Tying the rubber to the fork is definitely a two-person job! One person holds the fork and stretches the rubber (with the tab on the outside of the fork), and the other person wraps the floss tightly around the stretched rubber tubing and ties it. Don't spare the floss! Double it and use lots. And tie several knots as you go along the wrapping and tying process.

Little Fact: Poison ivy still has active oils up to 5 years after the plant's "death."

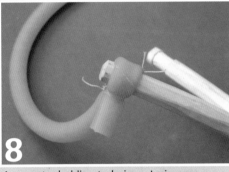

8

As an extra holding technique, I crisscross the floss several times across the front of the rubber and around the notched stem of the fork.

THE APPALACHIAN TRAIL

The Appalachian National Scenic Trail, the nation's longest marked footpath at 2,175 miles, originated eighty years ago as an idea in the head of Benton MacKaye, a forester and regional planner who worked for the U. S. Forest Service. He proposed the idea in his famous article, *An Appalachian Trail: A Project in Regional Planning.* Today, the Appalachian Trail—now known simply as the "A.T."—is a reality thanks to the work of thousands of volunteers, over 30 trail clubs, and many partnerships.

9

Securely tie the tubing to both sides of the leather pouch.

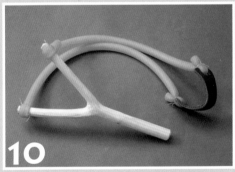

10

Done! Slingshots can be lots of fun and very useful, when they're used right. Some states may have special laws and regulations relating to slingshots. Be sure to check before putting yours to use. 'Nuff said!

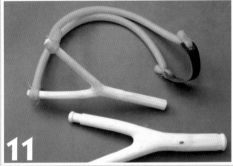

11

The particular fork that we used to make this slingshot, while of strong wood, is probably a bit thinner than I would normally use for this heavier gauge surgical tubing. The thicker fork at the bottom would be a better choice.

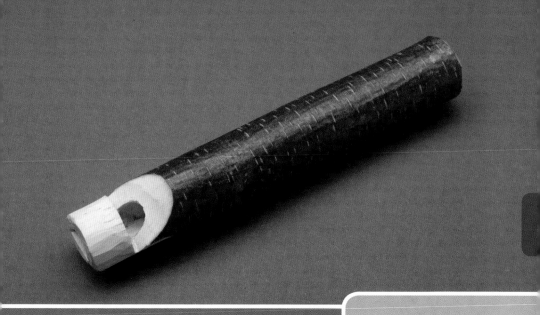

WHISTLE

MATERIALS:
- Knife
- 2 pieces of straight-grained wood of choice
- Sandpaper—a couple of grits on the fine to very fine side (150- and 220-grit would work).
- CA glue
- Drill

As I've traveled around the country, I can't even begin to tell you the number of folks who have told me how they used to make whistles from one kind of tree branch or another. Just about always the whistle was the "tap-the-bark/slide-it-off /notch-the-wood/slide-the-bark-back-on/and-blow" variety. Of course, only certain woods would work, and generally whistle manufacturing had to be done in the spring when the wood was very wet and the sap was running.

The directions I'll give in the following pages will be for a simple but fun whistle that can be made from a couple of round pieces of branch (or even a broom handle) any time of the year!

WHISTLE

1

Needed: a drill, two pieces of wood, and a knife. A larger drill bit than the one shown here would actually be better. Also, the wood for this type of whistle should be seasoned. (Green wood doesn't drill out cleanly and makes for a "fuzzy" hole—which doesn't work.

MAKING A GRASS WHISTLE

Remember whistling with a blade of grass when you were little? Most of us have forgotten how to do it. Here's a reminder:

1. Find a blade of grass approximately 1/4 inch wide.
2. Hold your thumbs together so that your nails are facing you.
3. Sandwich the blade of grass between your thumbs. Create a smooth, straight fit.
4. Place your lips over the opening between your thumbs and blow! You should hear a high-pitched whistle. Experiment with harder and softer blows for different sounds.

2

Drill a hole in the thick branch, stopping before you get to the end.

3

Remove the bark halfway around the hole end of the whistle.

4

Round and smooth the end.

5 Notch the barked side of the branch with repeated straight and diagonal cuts until you're about halfway through the hole you've drilled.

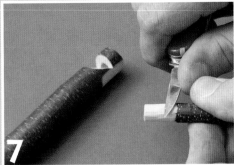

6 Select a smaller branch that has a diameter slightly greater than the diameter of the hole.

7 De-bark the end of the little branch.

WEATHER FOLKLORE

Did you know that according to ancient folklore, flower blossoms will close before a storm? Here are some other proverbs to help you predict what Mother Nature will do next:

Evening red and morning gray, sends the traveler on his way. Evening gray, morning red, brings the rain down on his head.

Expect the weather to be fair, when crows fly in pairs.

When ladybugs swarm, Expect a day that's warm.

Red sky at night, sailor's delight. Red sky in the morning, sailor take warning.

The hooting of an owl Says the weather will be foul.

Dew on the grass, Rain won't come to pass.

Halo around the moon, Rain or snow soon.

Rainbow in the morning Gives you fair warning. A rainbow afternoon, Good weather coming soon.

When the chairs squeak, It's about rain they speak.

Catchy drawer and sticky door, Coming rain will pour and pour.

A wind from the south Has rain in its mouth.

Little Tip: Get yourself into a sticky situation? Use baking soda to wash after handling sap.

WHISTLE

Make it into a little dowel that's flattened a bit on one side.

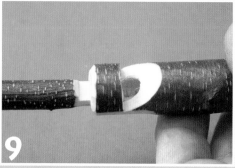

Fit the piece into the hole, flat side up and just reaching to the edge of the hole.

Cut the piece flush with the mouthpiece of the whistle.

Fill in any little crack with glue. Let the glue dry. Once the whistle is dry, blow! If the hole (sound chamber) is "clean as a whistle," it should work. If it's full of little wood fuzzies, like my first whistle was, it won't! I had to wait until my wood dried some more. Then, when I had the inside cleaned out, my whistle whistled!

USING SHADOWS TO DETERMINE DIRECTION

Whistles can be tools for signaling others, especially if you or they are lost. However, it never hurts to have some direction-finding strategies under your belt. Because the sun and the earth have a reasonably consistent relationship to each other, you can use shadows to determine direction.

1. Find a straight stick about one meter long and a clear, level piece of ground.

2. Push the stick into the ground.

3. Using a stone, branch, or similar instrument, mark the tip of the stick's shadow on the ground. This mark is always west, no matter where you are.

4. After 10 to 15 minutes, mark the tip of the stick's shadow again.

5. Draw a straight line through the two marks. This is your east-west line.

6. Stand so that the first (west) mark is at your left and the second (east) mark is at your right. The direction you are facing is north.

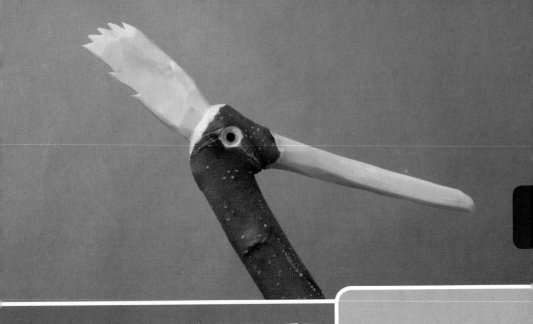

BACK SCRATCHER

MATERIALS:

- Knife
- Forked branch of choice
- Sandpaper—a couple of grits on the fine to very fine side (150- and 220-grit would work).
- Pencil, pen, or marker
- Acrylic paints of choice (optional)

I don't know about you, but in my opinion a backscratcher is an intensely useful and practical item. Granted, it may be a little tough to carry around throughout an average working day, but at least you can keep it next to your favorite recliner while you're watching the evening news or a good Duke/Carolina basketball game. With pinpoint precision, you can get at that itch in the middle of your back just below your shoulder blades without getting up to go scratch it on the corner of a kitchen cabinet. And you definitely don't want to ask your wife to scratch your back if she's an alumna of the team that's down by six points with 1.5 seconds left on the clock! Who knows what permanent damage she might do!

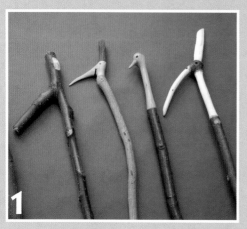

Naturally, there are different shapes and different degrees of sharpness, depending on the type of scratching you want to do. For superprecise, light, pinpoint scratching, you can carve a sharp-beaked, Dr. Seuss-type head, such as the red-crested critter in the middle. For harder, firmer, all-over scratching, I'd suggest a round-billed duck head. We'll use as our starting blank the piece on the left and aim for a broad-spectrum scratcher, sharp enough to be precise, but not so sharp as to tear clothing or skin when medium to firm pressure is applied.

Taper both sides of the topknot branch, cutting the same amount from both sides.

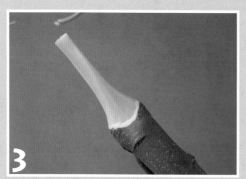

Remove the rest of the bark around the same branch.

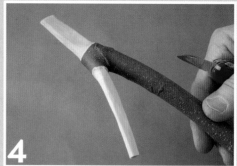

Remove the bark around the beak branch and taper the branch a little from both sides.

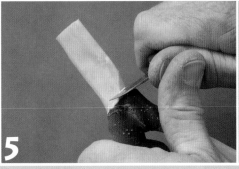
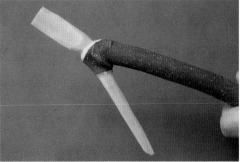

5 Notch around the base of the topknot to distinguish it from the top of the head, and sharpen the beak a bit.

6 Curve the top of the topknot slightly and sharpen it a bit from the sides.

7 Similar to the way you do the rooster's comb on the top of the poker (see page 29), make some V-notches in the topknot, or crest, or whatever you want to call it.

How to Prevent Blisters

With a new back scratcher, an itchy back is easily fixed. Other inconveniences campers are likely to get, like blisters, may be a little more difficult to care for. What's the best way to treat a blister? Don't get one! Here are a few tips:

- Remember—blisters are simply friction burns. The moment you feel the slightest rubbing in your shoe, stop and investigate. Find the wrinkle in your sock, the small pebble, the sand, or whatever it is, and get it out. If you think that the area will continue to rub, apply some moleskin as a preventative measure.
- Don't wear cotton socks. They soak up the sweat and moisture and will guarantee blisters. Instead wear sock liners of nylon or polypropylene under wool-and-nylon-blend socks. They're less abrasive, and they breathe or wick moisture away from your feet.
- Make sure your boots fit right; break in those new boots *before* hitting the trail.
- Try to limit your backpacking and hiking mileage.
- When you take a break to whittle, let your feet air out: take off your boots and socks, check your feet, and (if necessary) put on a pair of dry socks.

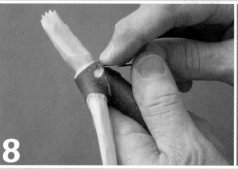

8 With the tip of your blade, remove the bark where you want the eyes.

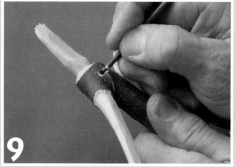

9 Paint the eyes. I like to use the sharpened tip of a brush handle.

10 Here's the working end of your backscratcher. Of course, you can add all kinds of detail and personality with some creative painting!

MAKING YOUR OWN FIRST-AID KIT

For everyday incidents, especially on the hiking trail, a first-aid kit is a must! Commercial kits are available and are probably a good place to start for a standard first-aid kit. Customize the kit according to your needs. If you're making the kit totally from scratch, be sure that you choose a container that's waterproof, easy to carry, and durable.

Some suggestions for the contents of your kit:

- Alcohol swabs
- Anesthetic ointment
- Antacid tablets
- Antibiotic ointment
- Antihistamines
- Bandages, in a variety of shapes and sizes
- Bee sting kit
- Cotton swabs
- Eye drops
- First-aid book
- Gauze pads
- Medical tape
- Moleskin
- Needle and thread
- Prescription medications for any special conditions
- Snakebite kit
- Surgical blades or knife
- Syringe
- Tweezers

MINIATURES CHALLENGE

Now that you've had some good practice and have completed some or all of the projects in this book, let me propose a fun challenge. Pick out some really small twigs and branches, and carve a variety of miniature pieces. When I think of all the carvings I do, I like my miniature ones the best. And, no, I don't think it's primarily a matter of patience, but rather of concentration. I suppose being quite nearsighted doesn't hurt either! Like many of you, I take my glasses off to see up close!

You can tell how small these projects are by comparing them to the dime.

More Great Project Books from Fox Chapel Publishing

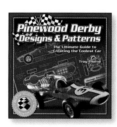
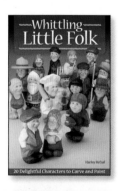
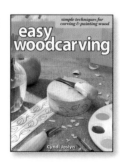